DOVER · THRIFT · EDITIONS

The Taming of the Shrew

WILLIAM SHAKESPEARE

DOVER PUBLICATIONS, INC.
Mineola, New York

DOVER THRIFT EDITIONS

GENERAL EDITOR: PAUL NEGRI
EDITOR OF THIS VOLUME: ADAM FROST

Copyright

Published in Canada by General Publishing Company, Ltd., 30 Lesmill Road, Don Mills, Toronto, Ontario.

Theatrical Rights

This Dover Thrift Edition may be used in its entirety, in adaptation or in any other way for theatrical productions, professional and amateur, in the United States, without fee, permission or acknowledgment. (This may not apply outside the United States, as copyright conditions may vary.)

Bibliographical Note

This Dover edition, first published in 1997, contains the unabridged text of *The Taming of the Shrew* as published in Volume IV of *The Caxton Edition of the Complete Works of William Shakespeare*, Caxton Publishing Company, London, n.d. The Note was prepared specially for this edition, and explanatory footnotes from the Caxton edition have been supplemented and revised.

Library of Congress Cataloging-in-Publication Data

Shakespeare, William, 1564–1616.
The taming of the shrew / William Shakespeare.
p. cm. — (Dover thrift editions)
ISBN 0-486-29765-9 (pbk.)
1. Married people — Italy — Padua — Drama. I. Title. II. Series.
[PR2832.A1 1997]
822.3'3 — dc21 97-6768
CIP

Manufactured in the United States of America
Dover Publications, Inc., 31 East 2nd Street, Mineola, N.Y. 11501

Note

IT IS FITTING THAT a play concerned with questions of identity and appearance should itself have a murky and uncertain history: such is the case with William Shakespeare's *The Taming of the Shrew* (c. 1592–1594). The diary of the Elizabethan playhouse owner Philip Henslowe notes a performance in June 1594 of "the tamynge of A shrowe," now thought to be a reference to Shakespeare's comedy despite the variant title. A problem of identification arises, however, due to the existence of an anonymously written play also called *The Taming of a Shrew*, which was entered into the Stationers' Register in May of 1594 and printed later that year. For a long time it was thought that *A Shrew* was Shakespeare's source, or that both plays were the offspring of a still older version, now lost. There is no evidence of a third version, however, and today it is considered most likely that *A Shrew* is either a direct imitation of Shakespeare's work by a rival dramatist, or a pirated version reconstructed from memory and rushed into print. It has also been suggested that, as the comedy is not mentioned by Francis Meres in his *Palladis Tamia* (1598), it might have once been called *Love's Labour's Won*, the mysterious and otherwise unknown play which Meres there attributes to Shakespeare. *The Taming of the Shrew*, as we know it today, seems not to have made its way into print until 1623, when it was included in the First Folio.

Contents

Dramatis Personæ

A Lord. CHRISTOPHER SLY, a tinker. Hostess, Page, Players, Huntsmen, and Servants.	Persons in the Induction.

BAPTISTA, a rich gentleman of Padua.
VINCENTIO, an old gentleman of Pisa.
LUCENTIO, son to Vincentio, in love with Bianca.
PETRUCHIO, a gentleman of Verona, a suitor to Katharina.

GREMIO, HORTENSIO,	suitors to Bianca.
TRANIO, BIONDELLO,	servants to Lucentio.
GRUMIO, CURTIS,	servants to Petruchio.

A Pedant.

KATHARINA, the shrew, BIANCA,	daughters to Baptista.

Widow.

Tailor, Haberdasher, and Servants attending on Baptista and Petruchio.

SCENE: *Padua, and Petruchio's country house.*

INDUCTION.

SCENE I. *Before an Alehouse on a Heath.*

Enter HOSTESS *and* SLY

SLY. I 'll pheeze[1] you, in faith.

HOST. A pair of stocks, you rogue!

SLY. Y' are a baggage: the Slys are no rogues; look in the chronicles; we came in with Richard Conqueror. Therefore paucas pallabris;[2] let the world slide: sessa![3]

HOST. You will not pay for the glasses you have burst?

SLY. No, not a denier. Go by, Jeronimy:[4] go to thy cold bed, and warm thee.

HOST. I know my remedy; I must go fetch the thirdborough.[5] [*Exit.*

SLY. Third, or fourth, or fifth borough, I 'll answer him by law: I 'll not budge an inch, boy: let him come, and kindly. [*Falls asleep.*

Horns winded. Enter a Lord *from hunting, with his train*

LORD. Huntsman, I charge thee, tender well my hounds:
Brach[6] Merriman, the poor cur is emboss'd;[7]
And couple Clowder with the deep-mouth'd brach.

[1] *pheeze*] beat.

[2] *paucas pallabris*] a corruption of the Spanish expression "pocas palabras," few words.

[3] *sessa*] an interjection of questionable meaning, possibly stemming from the Spanish "cessa," cease, be quiet.

[4] *Go by, Jeronimy*] a catch phrase made popular by Thomas Kyd's *Spanish Tragedy*, implying impatience or exasperation.

[5] *thirdborough*] constable.

[6] *Brach*] possibly a corruption of "Broach," bleed. In the following line the term is used in its usual sense, meaning a female scenting hound.

[7] *emboss'd*] foaming at the mouth from exhaustion.

Saw'st thou not, boy, how Silver made it good
At the hedge-corner, in the coldest fault?[8]
I would not lose the dog for twenty pound.
FIRST HUN. Why, Belman is as good as he, my lord;
He cried upon it at the merest loss,
And twice to-day pick'd out the dullest scent:
Trust me, I take him for the better dog.
LORD. Thou art a fool: if Echo were as fleet,
I would esteem him worth a dozen such.
But sup them well and look unto them all:
To-morrow I intend to hunt again.
FIRST HUN. I will, my lord.
LORD. What 's here? one dead, or drunk? See, doth he breathe?
SEC. HUN. He breathes, my lord. Were he not warm'd with ale,
This were a bed but cold to sleep so soundly.
LORD. O monstrous beast! how like a swine he lies!
Grim death, how foul and loathsome is thine image!
Sirs, I will practise on this drunken man.
What think you, if he were convey'd to bed,
Wrapp'd in sweet clothes, rings put upon his fingers,
A most delicious banquet by his bed,
And brave attendants near him when he wakes,
Would not the beggar then forget himself?
FIRST HUN. Believe me, lord, I think he cannot choose.
SEC. HUN. It would seem strange unto him when he waked.
LORD. Even as a flattering dream or worthless fancy.
Then take him up and manage well the jest:
Carry him gently to my fairest chamber
And hang it round with all my wanton pictures:
Balm his foul head in warm distilled waters
And burn sweet wood to make the lodging sweet:
Procure me music ready when he wakes,
To make a dulcet and a heavenly sound;
And if he chance to speak, be ready straight
And with a low submissive reverence

[8] *fault*] loss of scent.

Say "What is it your honour will command?"
Let one attend him with a silver basin
Full of rose-water and bestrew'd with flowers;
Another bear the ewer, the third a diaper,[9]
And say "Will 't please your lordship cool your hands?"
Some one be ready with a costly suit,
And ask him what apparel he will wear;
Another tell him of his hounds and horse,
And that his lady mourns at his disease:
Persuade him that he hath been lunatic;
And when he says he is, say that he dreams,
For he is nothing but a mighty lord.
This do and do it kindly, gentle sirs:
It will be pastime passing excellent,
If it be husbanded with modesty.[10]

FIRST HUN. My lord, I warrant you we will play our part,
As he shall think by our true diligence
He is no less than what we say he is.

LORD. Take him up gently and to bed with him;
And each one to his office when he wakes.
[*Some bear out Sly. A trumpet sounds.*
Sirrah, go see what trumpet 't is that sounds: [*Exit Servingman.*
Belike, some noble gentleman that means,
Travelling some journey, to repose him here.

Re-enter Servingman

How now! who is it?

SERV. An 't please your honour, players
That offer service to your lordship.

LORD. Bid them come near.

Enter Players

Now, fellows, you are welcome.

PLAYERS. We thank your honour.

[9] *diaper*] towel.
[10] *If . . . modesty*] If it be not overdone, if it be dealt with in moderation.

LORD. Do you intend to stay with me to-night?
A PLAYER. So please your lordship to accept our duty.
LORD. With all my heart. This fellow I remember,
Since once he play'd a farmer's eldest son:
'T was where you woo'd the gentlewoman so well:
I have forgot your name; but, sure, that part
Was aptly fitted and naturally perform'd.
A PLAYER. I think 't was Soto[11] that your honour means.
LORD. 'T is very true: thou didst it excellent.
Well, you are come to me in happy time;
The rather for I have some sport in hand
Wherein your cunning can assist me much.
There is a lord will hear you play to-night:
But I am doubtful of your modesties;
Lest over-eyeing of his odd behaviour, —
For yet his honour never heard a play, —
You break into some merry passion[12]
And so offend him; for I tell you, sirs,
If you should smile he grows impatient.
A PLAYER. Fear not, my lord: we can contain ourselves,
Were he the veriest antic[13] in the world.
LORD. Go, sirrah, take them to the buttery,
And give them friendly welcome every one:
Let them want nothing that my house affords.
[*Exit one with the Players.*
Sirrah, go you to Barthol'mew my page,
And see him dress'd in all suits like a lady:
That done, conduct him to the drunkard's chamber;
And call him "madam," do him obeisance.
Tell him from me, as he will win my love,
He bear himself with honourable action,
Such as he hath observed in noble ladies
Unto their lords, by them accomplished:

[11] *Soto*] doubtless a character in some unidentified Spanish or Italian play. The earliest English piece in which it is found is Beaumont and Fletcher's *Women Pleased* (1620?).
[12] *merry passion*] burst of merriment.
[13] *antic*] buffoon.

Such duty to the drunkard let him do
With soft low tongue and lowly courtesy,
And say, "What is 't your honour will command,
Wherein your lady and your humble wife
May show her duty and make known her love?"
And then with kind embracements, tempting kisses,
And with declining head into his bosom,
Bid him shed tears, as being overjoy'd
To see her noble lord restored to health,
Who for this seven years hath esteemed him
No better than a poor and loathsome beggar:
And if the boy have not a woman's gift
To rain a shower of commanded tears,
An onion will do well for such a shift,
Which in a napkin being close convey'd
Shall in despite enforce a watery eye.
See this dispatch'd with all the haste thou canst:
Anon I 'll give thee more instructions. [*Exit a Servingman.*
I know the boy will well usurp the grace,
Voice, gait and action of a gentlewoman:
I long to hear him call the drunkard husband,
And how my men will stay themselves from laughter
When they do homage to this simple peasant.
I 'll in to counsel them; haply my presence
May well abate the over-merry spleen
Which otherwise would grow into extremes. [*Exeunt.*

SCENE II. *A Bedchamber in the Lord's House.*

Enter aloft SLY, *with* Attendants; *some with apparel, others with basin and ewer and other appurtenances, and* Lord

SLY. For God's sake, a pot of small ale.
FIRST SERV. Will 't please your lordship drink a cup of sack?[1]

[1] *small ale . . . sack*] weak beer . . . sweet Spanish wine.

SEC. SERV. Will 't please your honour taste of these conserves?

THIRD SERV. What raiment will your honour wear to-day?

SLY. I am Christophero Sly; call not me "honour" nor "lordship:" I ne'er drank sack in my life; and if you give me any conserves, give me conserves of beef: ne'er ask me what raiment I 'll wear; for I have no more doublets than backs, no more stockings than legs, nor no more shoes than feet; nay, sometime more feet than shoes, or such shoes as my toes look through the overleather.

LORD. Heaven cease this idle humour in your honour!
O, that a mighty man of such descent,
Of such possessions and so high esteem,
Should be infused with so foul a spirit!

SLY. What, would you make me mad? Am not I Christopher Sly, old Sly's son of Burton-heath, by birth a pedlar, by education a card-maker, by transmutation a bear-herd, and now by present profession a tinker? Ask Marian Hacket, the fat ale-wife of Wincot, if she know me not: if she say I am not fourteen pence on the score for sheer ale, score me up for the lyingest knave in Christendom. What! I am not bestraught: here 's —

THIRD SERV. O, this it is that makes your lady mourn!

SEC. SERV. O, this is it that makes your servants droop!

LORD. Hence comes it that your kindred shuns your house,
As beaten hence by your strange lunacy.
O noble lord, bethink thee of thy birth,
Call home thy ancient thoughts from banishment,
And banish hence these abject lowly dreams.
Look how thy servants do attend on thee,
Each in his office ready at thy beck.
Wilt thou have music? hark! Apollo plays, [*Music.*
And twenty caged nightingales do sing:
Or wilt thou sleep? we 'll have thee to a couch
Softer and sweeter than the lustful bed
On purpose trimm'd up for Semiramis.[2]
Say thou wilt walk; we will bestrew the ground:

[2] *Semiramis*] Queen of Assyria, proverbial for her voluptuousness and cruelty.

Or wilt thou ride? thy horses shall be trapp'd,
Their harness studded all with gold and pearl.
Dost thou love hawking? thou hast hawks will soar
Above the morning lark: or wilt thou hunt?
Thy hounds shall make the welkin answer them,
And fetch shrill echoes from the hollow earth.

FIRST SERV. Say thou wilt course; thy greyhounds are as swift
As breathed stags, ay, fleeter than the roe.

SEC. SERV. Dost thou love pictures? we will fetch thee straight
Adonis painted by a running brook,
And Cytherea[3] all in sedges hid,
Which seem to move and wanton with her breath,
Even as the waving sedges play with wind.

LORD. We 'll show thee Io[4] as she was a maid
And how she was beguiled and surprised,
As lively painted as the deed was done.

THIRD SERV. Or Daphne roaming through a thorny wood,
Scratching her legs that one shall swear she bleeds,
And at that sight shall sad Apollo weep,
So workmanly the blood and tears are drawn.

LORD. Thou art a lord and nothing but a lord:
Thou hast a lady far more beautiful
Than any woman in this waning age.

FIRST SERV. And till the tears that she hath shed for thee
Like envious floods o'er-run her lovely face,
She was the fairest creature in the world;
And yet she is inferior to none.

SLY. Am I a lord? and have I such a lady?
Or do I dream? or have I dream'd till now?
I do not sleep: I see, I hear, I speak;
I smell sweet savours and I feel soft things:
Upon my life, I am a lord indeed,
And not a tinker nor Christophero Sly.
Well, bring our lady hither to our sight;

[3] *Cytherea*] Venus.
[4] *Io*] one of Jove's mistresses, changed by the jealous Juno into a heifer.

And once again, a pot o' the smallest ale.
SEC. SERV. Will 't please your mightiness to wash your hands?
O, how we joy to see your wit restored!
O, that once more you knew but what you are!
These fifteen years you have been in a dream;
Or when you waked, so waked as if you slept.
SLY. These fifteen years! by my fay, a goodly nap.
But did I never speak of all that time?
FIRST SERV. O, yes, my lord, but very idle words:
For though you lay here in this goodly chamber,
Yet would you say ye were beaten out of door;
And rail upon the hostess of the house;
And say you would present her at the leet,[5]
Because she brought stone jugs and no seal'd quarts:[6]
Sometimes you would call out for Cicely Hacket.
SLY. Ay, the woman's maid of the house.
THIRD SERV. Why, sir, you know no house nor no such maid,
Nor no such men as you have reckon'd up,
As Stephen Sly and old John Naps of Greece[7]
And Peter Turph and Henry Pimpernell
And twenty more such names and men as these
Which never were nor no man ever saw.
SLY. Now Lord be thanked for my good amends!
ALL. Amen.
SLY. I thank thee: thou shalt not lose by it.

Enter the Page *as a lady, attended*

PAGE. How fares my noble lord?
SLY. Marry, I fare well; for here is cheer enough.
Where is my wife?
PAGE. Here, noble lord: what is thy will with her?
SLY. Are you my wife and will not call me husband?

[5] *leet*] a manor court.
[6] *seal'd quarts*] quart pots certified by an official stamp.
[7] *Greece*] Doubtless a misreading of "Greet," a hamlet in Gloucestershire, not far from Stratford-on-Avon.

My men should call me "lord": I am your good-man.
PAGE. My husband and my lord, my lord and husband;
I am your wife in all obedience.
SLY. I know it well. What must I call her?
LORD. Madam.
SLY. Al'ce madam, or Joan madam?
LORD. "Madam" and nothing else: so lords call ladies.
SLY. Madam wife, they say that I have dream'd
And slept above some fifteen year or more.
PAGE. Ay, and the time seems thirty unto me,
Being all this time abandon'd from your bed.
SLY. 'T is much. Servants, leave me and her alone.
Madam, undress you and come now to bed.
PAGE. Thrice-noble lord, let me entreat of you
To pardon me yet for a night or two;
Or, if not so, until the sun be set:
For your physicians have expressly charged,
In peril to incur your former malady,
That I should yet absent me from your bed:
I hope this reason stands for my excuse.
SLY. Ay, it stands so that I may hardly tarry so long. But I would be loath to fall into my dreams again: I will therefore tarry in despite of the flesh and the blood.

Enter a Messenger

MESS. Your honour's players, hearing your amendment,
Are come to play a pleasant comedy;
For so your doctors hold it very meet,
Seeing too much sadness hath congeal'd your blood,
And melancholy is the nurse of frenzy:
Therefore they thought it good you hear a play
And frame your mind to mirth and merriment,
Which bars a thousand harms and lengthens life.
SLY. Marry, I will, let them play it. Is not a comonty[8] a Christmas gambold or a tumbling-trick?

[8] *comonty*] comedy.

PAGE. No, my good lord; it is more pleasing stuff.

SLY. What, household stuff?

PAGE. It is a kind of history.

SLY. Well, we 'll see 't. Come, madame wife, sit by my side and let the world slip: we shall ne'er be younger.

Flourish

ACT I.

SCENE I. *Padua. A Public Place.*

Enter LUCENTIO *and his man* TRANIO

LUC. Tranio, since for the great desire I had
To see fair Padua, nursery of arts,[1]
I am arrived for fruitful Lombardy,
The pleasant garden of great Italy;
And by my father's love and leave am arm'd
With his good will and thy good company,
My trusty servant, well approved in all,
Here let us breathe and haply institute
A course of learning and ingenious studies.
Pisa renowned for grave citizens
Gave me my being and my father first,
A merchant of great traffic through the world,
Vincentio, come of the Bentivolii.
Vincentio's son brought up in Florence
It shall become to serve all hopes conceived,
To deck his fortune with his virtuous deeds:
And therefore, Tranio, for the time I study,
Virtue and that part of philosophy
Will I apply that treats of happiness
By virtue specially to be achieved.
Tell me thy mind; for I have Pisa left
And am to Padua come, as he that leaves

[1] *nursery of arts*] the university at Padua was one of the most renowned during Shakespeare's time.

A shallow plash to plunge him in the deep,
And with satiety seeks to quench his thirst.

TRA. *Mi perdonato*, gentle master mine,
I am in all affected as yourself;
Glad that you thus continue your resolve
To suck the sweets of sweet philosophy.
Only, good master, while we do admire
This virtue and this moral discipline,
Let 's be no stoics nor no stocks,[2] I pray;
Or so devote to Aristotle's checks[3]
As Ovid be an outcast quite abjured:
Balk logic[4] with acquaintance that you have,
And practise rhetoric in your common talk;
Music and poesy use to quicken you;
The mathematics and the metaphysics,
Fall to them as you find your stomach serves you;
No profit grows where is no pleasure ta'en:
In brief, sir, study what you most affect.

LUC. Gramercies, Tranio, well dost thou advise.
If, Biondello, thou wert come ashore,
We could at once put us in readiness,
And take a lodging fit to entertain
Such friends as time in Padua shall beget.
But stay a while: what company is this?

TRA. Master, some show to welcome us to town.

Enter BAPTISTA, KATHARINA, BIANCA, GREMIO, *and* HORTENSIO. LUCENTIO *and* TRANIO *stand by*

BAP. Gentlemen, importune me no farther,
For how I firmly am resolved you know;
That is, not to bestow my youngest daughter
Before I have a husband for the elder:
If either of you both love Katharina,

[2] *stocks*] senseless people.
[3] *checks*] rebukes, reproofs.
[4] *Balk logic*] Argue in the manner of logicians.

Because I know you well and love you well,
Leave shall you have to court her at your pleasure.
GRE. [*Aside*] To cart[5] her rather: she 's too rough for me.
There, there, Hortensio, will you any wife?
KATH. I pray you, sir, is it your will
To make a stale of me amongst these mates?[6]
HOR. Mates, maid! how mean you that? no mates for you,
Unless you were of gentler, milder mould.
KATH. I' faith, sir, you shall never need to fear:
I wis it is not half way to her heart;
But if it were, doubt not her care should be
To comb your noddle with a three-legg'd stool
And paint your face and use you like a fool.
HOR. From all such devils, good Lord deliver us!
GRE. And me too, good Lord!
TRA. Husht, master! here 's some good pastime toward:
That wench is stark mad or wonderful froward.
LUC. But in the other's silence do I see
Maid's mild behaviour and sobriety.
Peace, Tranio!
TRA. Well said, master; mum! and gaze your fill.
BAP. Gentlemen, that I may soon make good
What I have said, Bianca, get you in:
And let it not displease thee, good Bianca,
For I will love thee ne'er the less, my girl.
KATH. A pretty peat![7] it is best
Put finger in the eye, an she knew why.
BIAN. Sister, content you in my discontent.
Sir, to your pleasure humbly I subscribe:
My books and instruments shall be my company,
On them to look and practise by myself.
LUC. Hark, Tranio! thou may'st hear Minerva speak.
HOR. Signior Baptista, will you be so strange?

[5] *cart*] to expose in a cart, by way of public punishment.
[6] *stale . . . mates*] common harlot . . . coarse fellows.
[7] *peat*] archaic form of "pet," darling.

Sorry am I that our good will effects
Bianca's grief.

GRE. Why will you mew her up,[8]
Signior Baptista, for this fiend of hell,
And make her bear the penance of her tongue?

BAP. Gentlemen, content ye; I am resolved:
Go in, Bianca: [*Exit Bianca.*
And for I know she taketh most delight
In music, instruments and poetry,
Schoolmasters will I keep within my house,
Fit to instruct her youth. If you, Hortensio,
Or Signior Gremio, you, know any such,
Prefer them hither; for to cunning men
I will be very kind, and liberal
To mine own children in good bringing-up.
And so farewell. Katharina, you may stay;
For I have more to commune with Bianca. [*Exit.*

KATH. Why, and I trust I may go too, may I not?
What, shall I be appointed hours; as though, belike,
I knew not what to take, and what to leave, ha? [*Exit.*

GRE. You may go to the devil's dam: your gifts are so good, here 's none will hold you. Their love is not so great, Hortensio, but we may blow our nails together,[9] and fast it fairly out: our cake 's dough on both sides. Farewell: yet, for the love I bear my sweet Bianca, if I can by any means light on a fit man to teach her that wherein she delights, I will wish[10] him to her father.

HOR. So will I, Signior Gremio: but a word, I pray. Though the nature of our quarrel yet never brooked parle,[11] know now, upon advice, it toucheth us both, that we may yet again have access to our fair mistress, and be happy rivals in Bianca's love, to labour and effect one thing specially.

GRE. What 's that, I pray?

HOR. Marry, sir, to get a husband for her sister.

[8] *mew her up*] coop her up.

[9] *we may blow our nails together*] we may twiddle our thumbs.

[10] *wish*] recommend.

[11] *brooked parle*] tolerated conference.

GRE. A husband! a devil.

HOR. I say, a husband.

GRE. I say, a devil. Thinkest thou, Hortensio, though her father be very rich, any man is so very a fool to be married to hell?

HOR. Tush, Gremio, though it pass your patience and mine to endure her loud alarums, why, man, there be good fellows in the world, an a man could light on them, would take her with all her faults, and money enough.

GRE. I cannot tell; but I had as lief take her dowry with this condition, to be whipped at the high-cross[12] every morning.

HOR. Faith, as you say, there 's small choice in rotten apples. But come; since this bar in law makes us friends, it shall be so far forth friendly maintained till by helping Baptista's eldest daughter to a husband we set his youngest free for a husband, and then have to 't afresh. Sweet Bianca! Happy man be his dole![13] He that runs fastest gets the ring.[14] How say you, Signior Gremio?

GRE. I am agreed; and would I had given him the best horse in Padua to begin his wooing that would thoroughly woo her, wed her and bed her and rid the house of her! Come on.

[*Exeunt Gremio and Hortensio.*

TRA. I pray, sir, tell me, is it possible
That love should of a sudden take such hold?

LUC. O Tranio, till I found it to be true,
I never thought it possible or likely;
But see, while idly I stood looking on,
I found the effect of love in idleness:
And now in plainness do confess to thee,
That art to me as secret and as dear
As Anna to the Queen of Carthage[15] was,
Tranio, I burn, I pine, I perish, Tranio,
If I achieve not this young modest girl.
Counsel me, Tranio, for I know thou canst;
Assist me, Tranio, for I know thou wilt.

[12] *high-cross*] the cross usually found set up in the market place of a town.
[13] *dole*] lot, portion.
[14] *the ring*] the prize in a running match.
[15] *Anna . . . Carthage*] Anna was the sister of and confidante to Dido, Queen of Carthage.

TRA. Master, it is no time to chide you now;
Affection is not rated[16] from the heart:
If love have touch'd you, nought remains but so,
"Redime te captum quam queas minimo."[17]

LUC. Gramercies, lad, go forward; this contents:
The rest will comfort, for thy counsel 's sound.

TRA. Master, you look'd so longly on the maid,
Perhaps you mark'd not what 's the pith of all.

LUC. O yes, I saw sweet beauty in her face,
Such as the daughter of Agenor[18] had,
That made great Jove to humble him to her hand,
When with his knees he kiss'd the Cretan strond.

TRA. Saw you no more? mark'd you not how her sister
Began to scold and raise up such a storm
That mortal ears might hardly endure the din?

LUC. Tranio, I saw her coral lips to move
And with her breath she did perfume the air:
Sacred and sweet was all I saw in her.

TRA. Nay, then, 't is time to stir him from his trance.
I pray, awake, sir: if you love the maid,
Bend thoughts and wits to achieve her. Thus it stands:
Her elder sister is so curst and shrewd
That till the father rid his hands of her,
Master, your love must live a maid at home;
And therefore has he closely mew'd her up,
Because she will not be annoy'd with suitors.

LUC. Ah, Tranio, what a cruel father 's he!
But art thou not advised, he took some care
To get her cunning schoolmasters to instruct her?

TRA. Ay, marry, am I, sir; and now 't is plotted.

LUC. I have it, Tranio.

TRA. Master, for my hand,
Both our inventions meet and jump in one.

[16] *rated*] scolded, driven out by chiding.
[17] *"Redime . . . minimo"*] "Redeem yourself from captivity as cheaply as possible."
[18] *daughter of Agenor*] Europa.

LUC. Tell me thine first.
TRA. You will be schoolmaster
And undertake the teaching of the maid:
That 's your device.
LUC. It is: may it be done?
TRA. Not possible; for who shall bear your part,
And be in Padua here Vincentio's son;
Keep house and ply his book, welcome his friends,
Visit his countrymen and banquet them?
LUC. Basta;[19] content thee, for I have it full.
We have not yet been seen in any house,
Nor can we be distinguish'd by our faces
For man or master; then it follows thus;
Thou shalt be master, Tranio, in my stead,
Keep house and port[20] and servants, as I should:
I will some other be; some Florentine,
Some Neapolitan, or meaner man of Pisa.
'T is hatch'd and shall be so: Tranio, at once
Uncase thee; take my colour'd hat and cloak:
When Biondello comes, he waits on thee;
But I will charm him first to keep his tongue.
TRA. So had you need.
In brief, sir, sith it your pleasure is,
And I am tied to be obedient,
For so your father charged me at our parting;
"Be serviceable to my son," quoth he,
Although I think 't was in another sense;
I am content to be Lucentio,
Because so well I love Lucentio.
LUC. Tranio, be so, because Lucentio loves:
And let me be a slave, to achieve that maid
Whose sudden sight hath thrall'd my wounded eye.
Here comes the rogue.

Enter BIONDELLO

[19] *Basta*] Enough.
[20] *port*] magnificence or pomp.

Sirrah, where have you been?

BION. Where have I been! Nay, how now! where are you? Master, has my fellow Tranio stolen your clothes? Or you stolen his? or both? pray, what 's the news?

LUC. Sirrah, come hither: 't is no time to jest,
And therefore frame your manners to the time.
Your fellow Tranio here, to save my life,
Puts my apparel and my countenance on,
And I for my escape have put on his;
For in a quarrel since I came ashore
I kill'd a man and fear I was descried:
Wait you on him, I charge you, as becomes,
While I make way from hence to save my life:
You understand me?

BION. I, sir! ne'er a whit.

LUC. And not a jot of Tranio in your mouth:
Tranio is changed into Lucentio.

BION. The better for him: would I were so too!

TRA. So could I, faith, boy, to have the next wish after,
That Lucentio indeed had Baptista's youngest daughter.
But, sirrah, not for my sake, but your master's, I advise
You use your manners discreetly in all kind of companies:
When I am alone, why, then I am Tranio;
But in all places else your master Lucentio.

LUC. Tranio, let 's go: one thing more rests, that thyself execute, to make one among these wooers: if thou ask me why, sufficeth, my reasons are both good and weighty. [*Exeunt.*

The presenters[21] *above speak*

FIRST SERV. My lord, you nod; you do not mind the play.

SLY. Yes, by Saint Anne, do I. A good matter, surely: comes there any more of it?

PAGE. My lord, 't is but begun.

SLY. 'T is a very excellent piece of work, madam lady: would 't were done! [*They sit and mark.*

[21] *presenters*] those who present the Induction.

SCENE II. *Padua. Before Hortensio's House.*

Enter PETRUCHIO *and his man* GRUMIO

PET. Verona, for a while I take my leave,
To see my friends in Padua, but of all
My best beloved and approved friend,
Hortensio; and I trow this is his house.
Here, sirrah Grumio; knock, I say.

GRU. Knock, sir! whom should I knock? is there any man has rebused your worship?

PET. Villain, I say, knock me here[1] soundly.

GRU. Knock you here, sir! why, sir, what am I, sir, that I should knock you here, sir?

PET. Villain, I say, knock me at this gate
And rap me well, or I 'll knock your knave's pate.

GRU. My master is grown quarrelsome. I should knock you first,
And then I know after who comes by the worst.

PET. Will it not be?
Faith, sirrah, an you 'll not knock, I 'll ring it;
I 'll try how you can *sol, fa,* and sing it.
[*He wrings him by the ears.*

GRU. Help, masters, help! my master is mad.

PET. Now, knock when I bid you, sirrah villain!

Enter HORTENSIO

HOR. How now! what 's the matter? My old friend Grumio! and my good friend Petruchio! How do you all at Verona?

PET. Signior Hortensio, come you to part the fray?
"Con tutto il core ben trovato,"[2] may I say.

HOR. "Alla nostra casa ben venuto, molto honorato signor mio Petrucio."[3]

[1] *knock me here*] knock for me here.
[2] *"Con . . . trovato"*] "With all my heart, well met."
[3] *"Alla . . . Petrucio"*] "Welcome to our house, my much honored Petrucio."

Rise, Grumio, rise: we will compound this quarrel.

GRU. Nay, 't is no matter, sir, what he 'leges in Latin. If this be not a lawful cause for me to leave his service, look you, sir, he bid me knock him and rap him soundly, sir: well, was it fit for a servant to use his master so, being perhaps, for aught I see, two-and-thirty, a pip out?[4]
Whom would to God I had well knock'd at first,
Then had not Grumio come by the worst.

PET. A senseless villain! Good Hortensio,
I bade the rascal knock upon your gate
And could not get him for my heart to do it.

GRU. Knock at the gate! O heavens! Spake you not these words plain, "Sirrah, knock me here, rap me here, knock me well, and knock me soundly"? And come you now with, "knocking at the gate"?

PET. Sirrah, be gone, or talk not, I advise you.

HOR. Petruchio, patience; I am Grumio's pledge:
Why, this 's a heavy chance 'twixt him and you,
Your ancient, trusty, pleasant servant Grumio.
And tell me now, sweet friend, what happy gale
Blows you to Padua here from old Verona?

PET. Such wind as scatters young men through the world,
To seek their fortunes farther than at home,
Where small experience grows. But in a few,
Signior Hortensio, thus it stands with me:
Antonio, my father, is deceased;
And I have thrust myself into this maze,
Haply to wive and thrive as best I may:
Crowns in my purse I have and goods at home,
And so am come abroad to see the world.

HOR. Petruchio, shall I then come roundly[5] to thee,
And wish thee to a shrewd ill-favour'd wife?
Thou 'ldst thank me but a little for my counsel:
And yet I 'll promise thee she shall be rich,

[4] *two-and-thirty, a pip out*] Pip is a spot on playing cards. The allusion is to an old card game, called "bone ace," or "one and thirty."

[5] *come roundly*] speak bluntly or outspokenly.

And very rich: but thou 'rt too much my friend,
And I 'll not wish thee to her.

PET. Signior Hortensio, 'twixt such friends as we
Few words suffice; and therefore, if thou know
One rich enough to be Petruchio's wife,
As wealth is burden[6] of my wooing dance,
Be she as foul as was Florentius' love,[7]
As old as Sibyl,[8] and as curst and shrewd
As Socrates' Xanthippe, or a worse,
She moves me not, or not removes, at least,
Affection's edge in me, were she as rough
As are the swelling Adriatic seas:
I come to wive it wealthily in Padua;
If wealthily, then happily in Padua.

GRU. Nay, look you, sir, he tells you flatly what his mind is: why, give him gold enough and marry him to a puppet or an aglet-baby; or an old trot with ne'er a tooth in her head, though she have as many diseases as two and fifty horses: why, nothing comes amiss, so money comes withal.

HOR. Petruchio, since we are stepp'd thus far in,
I will continue that I broach'd in jest.
I can, Petruchio, help thee to a wife
With wealth enough and young and beauteous,
Brought up as best becomes a gentlewoman:
Her only fault, and that is faults enough,
Is that she is intolerable curst
And shrewd and froward, so beyond all measure,
That, were my state far worser than it is,
I would not wed her for a mine of gold.

PET. Hortensio, peace! thou know'st not gold's effect:
Tell me her father's name and 't is enough;

[6] *burden*] musical accompaniment.

[7] *Florentius' love*] Gower in his *Confessio Amantis* tells the old story of the knight Florent or Florentius, who swore to marry a hideous hag in consideration of her giving him the answer to a riddle, which he was pledged either to solve or to die.

[8] *Sibyl*] ancient prophetess, to whom Apollo gave as many years of life as she held grains of sand in her hand.

For I will board her, though she chide as loud
As thunder when the clouds in autumn crack.

HOR. Her father is Baptista Minola,
An affable and courteous gentleman:
Her name is Katharina Minola,
Renown'd in Padua for her scolding tongue.

PET. I know her father, though I know not her;
And he knew my deceased father well.
I will not sleep, Hortensio, till I see her;
And therefore let me be thus bold with you
To give you over[9] at this first encounter,
Unless you will accompany me thither.

GRU. I pray you, sir, let him go while the humour lasts. O' my word, an she knew him as well as I do, she would think scolding would do little good upon him: she may perhaps call him half a score knaves or so: why, that 's nothing; an he begin once, he 'll rail in his rope-tricks.[10] I 'll tell you what, sir, an she stand him but a little, he will throw a figure[11] in her face and so disfigure her with it that she shall have no more eyes to see withal than a cat.[12] You know him not, sir.

HOR. Tarry, Petruchio, I must go with thee;
For in Baptista's keep my treasure is:
He hath the jewel of my life in hold,
His youngest daughter, beautiful Bianca;
And her withholds from me and other more,
Suitors to her and rivals in my love;
Supposing it a thing impossible,
For those defects I have before rehearsed,
That ever Katharina will be woo'd;
Therefore this order hath Baptista ta'en,
That none shall have access unto Bianca

[9] *give you over*] abandon you.

[10] *rope-tricks*] The use of "figure (of speech)" in the next sentence suggests that Grumio is mispronouncing "rhetoric" when he employs the word "rope-tricks."

[11] *figure*] a figure of speech.

[12] *a cat*] The cat was commonly reputed to be purblind or blear-eyed by day, though well able to see in the dark.

Till Katharine the curst have got a husband.
GRU. Katharine the curst!
A title for a maid of all titles the worst.
HOR. Now shall my friend Petruchio do me grace;
And offer me disguised in sober robes
To old Baptista as a schoolmaster
Well seen in music, to instruct Bianca;
That so I may, by this device, at least
Have leave and leisure to make love to her,
And unsuspected court her by herself.
GRU. Here 's no knavery! See, to beguile the old folks, how the young folks lay their heads together!

Enter GREMIO, *and* LUCENTIO *disguised*

Master, master, look about you: who goes there, ha?
HOR. Peace, Grumio! it is the rival of my love.
Petruchio, stand by a while.
GRU. A proper stripling and an amorous!
GRE. O, very well; I have perused the note.
Hark you, sir; I 'll have them very fairly bound:
All books of love, see that at any hand;
And see you read no other lectures to her:
You understand me: over and beside
Signior Baptista's liberality,
I 'll mend it with a largess. Take your paper too,
And let me have them very well perfumed:
For she is sweeter than perfume itself
To whom they go to. What will you read to her?
LUC. Whate'er I read to her, I 'll plead for you
As for my patron, stand you so assured,
As firmly as yourself were still in place:
Yea, and perhaps with more successful words
Than you, unless you were a scholar, sir.
GRE. O this learning, what a thing it is!
GRU. O this woodcock, what an ass it is!
PET. Peace, sirrah!
HOR. Grumio, mum! God save you, Signior Gremio.

GRE. And you are well met, Signior Hortensio.
Trow you whither I am going? To Baptista Minola.
I promised to inquire carefully
About a schoolmaster for the fair Bianca:
And by good fortune I have lighted well
On this young man, for learning and behaviour
Fit for her turn, well read in poetry
And other books, good ones, I warrant ye.
HOR. 'T is well; and I have met a gentleman
Hath promised me to help me to another,
A fine musician to instruct our mistress;
So shall I no whit be behind in duty
To fair Bianca, so beloved of me.
GRE. Beloved of me; and that my deeds shall prove.
GRU. And that his bags shall prove.
HOR. Gremio, 't is now no time to vent our love:
Listen to me, and if you speak me fair,
I 'll tell you news indifferent good for either.
Here is a gentleman whom by chance I met,
Upon agreement from us to his liking,
Will undertake to woo curst Katharine,
Yea, and to marry her, if her dowry please.
GRE. So said, so done, is well.
Hortensio, have you told him all her faults?
PET. I know she is an irksome brawling scold:
If that be all, masters, I hear no harm.
GRE. No, say'st me so, friend? What countryman?
PET. Born in Verona, old Antonio's son:
My father dead, my fortune lives for me;
And I do hope good days and long to see.
GRE. O sir, such a life, with such a wife, were strange!
But if you have a stomach, to 't i' God's name:
You shall have me assisting you in all.
But will you woo this wild-cat?
PET. Will I live?
GRU. Will he woo her? ay, or I 'll hang her.
PET. Why came I hither but to that intent?

Think you a little din can daunt mine ears?
Have I not in my time heard lions roar?
Have I not heard the sea puff'd up with winds
Rage like an angry boar chafed with sweat?
Have I not heard great ordnance in the field,
And heaven's artillery thunder in the skies?
Have I not in a pitched battle heard
Loud 'larums, neighing steeds, and trumpets' clang?
And do you tell me of a woman's tongue,
That gives not half so great a blow to hear
As will a chestnut in a farmer's fire?
Tush, tush! fear boys with bugs.[13]

GRU. For he fears none.

GRE. Hortensio, hark:
This gentleman is happily arrived,
My mind presumes, for his own good and ours.

HOR. I promised we would be contributors
And bear his charge of wooing, whatsoe'er.

GRE. And so we will, provided that he win her.

GRU. I would I were as sure of a good dinner.

Enter TRANIO *brave, and* BIONDELLO

TRA. Gentlemen, God save you. If I may be bold,
Tell me, I beseech you, which is the readiest way
To the house of Signior Baptista Minola?

BION. He that has the two fair daughters: is 't he you mean?

TRA. Even he, Biondello.

GRE. Hark you, sir; you mean not her to —

TRA. Perhaps, him and her, sir: what have you to do?

PET. Not her that chides, sir, at any hand, I pray.

TRA. I love no chiders, sir. Biondello, let 's away.

LUC. Well begun, Tranio.

HOR. Sir, a word ere you go;
Are you a suitor to the maid you talk of, yea or no?

TRA. And if I be, sir, is it any offence?

[13] *fear . . . bugs*] frighten boys with bugbears.

GRE. No; if without more words you will get you hence.
TRA. Why, sir, I pray, are not the streets as free
For me as for you?
GRE. But so is not she.
TRA. For what reason, I beseech you?
GRE. For this reason, if you 'll know,
That she 's the choice love of Signior Gremio.
HOR. That she 's the chosen of Signior Hortensio.
TRA. Softly, my masters! if you be gentlemen,
Do me this right; hear me with patience.
Baptista is a noble gentleman,
To whom my father is not all unknown;
And were his daughter fairer than she is,
She may more suitors have and me for one.
Fair Leda's daughter[14] had a thousand wooers;
Then well one more may fair Bianca have:
And so she shall; Lucentio shall make one,
Though Paris came in hope to speed alone.
GRE. What, this gentleman will out-talk us all!
LUC. Sir, give him head: I know he 'll prove a jade.[15]
PET. Hortensio, to what end are all these words?
HOR. Sir, let me be so bold as ask you,
Did you yet ever see Baptista's daughter?
TRA. No, sir; but hear I do that he hath two,
The one as famous for a scolding tongue
As is the other for beauteous modesty.
PET. Sir, sir, the first 's for me; let her go by.
GRE. Yea, leave that labour to great Hercules;
And let it be more than Alcides'[16] twelve.
PET. Sir, understand you this of me in sooth:
The youngest daughter whom you hearken for
Her father keeps from all access of suitors;
And will not promise her to any man

[14] *Fair Leda's daughter*] Helen of Troy.
[15] *jade*] a horse that cannot be trusted.
[16] *Alcides'*] Hercules'.

Until the elder sister first be wed:
The younger then is free and not before.

TRA. If it be so, sir, that you are the man
Must stead us all and me amongst the rest;
And if you break the ice and do this feat,
Achieve the elder, set the younger free
For our access, whose hap shall be to have her
Will not so graceless be to be ingrate.

HOR. Sir, you say well and well you do conceive;
And since you do profess to be a suitor,
You must, as we do, gratify this gentleman,
To whom we all rest generally beholding.

TRA. Sir, I shall not be slack: in sign whereof,
Please ye we may contrive[17] this afternoon,
And quaff carouses to our mistress' health,
And do as adversaries do in law,
Strive mightily, but eat and drink as friends.

GRU. BION. O excellent motion! Fellows, let 's be gone.

HOR. The motion 's good indeed and be it so,
Petruchio, I shall be your ben venuto.[18] [*Exeunt.*

[17] *contrive*] spend.
[18] *ben venuto*] welcome; Hortensio is host to Petruchio.

ACT II.

SCENE I. *Padua. A Room in Baptista's House.*

Enter KATHARINA *and* BIANCA

BIAN. Good sister, wrong me not, nor wrong yourself,
To make a bondmaid and a slave of me;
That I disdain: but for these other gawds,[1]
Unbind my hands, I 'll pull them off myself,
Yea, all my raiment, to my petticoat;
Or what you will command me will I do,
So well I know my duty to my elders.

KATH. Of all thy suitors, here I charge thee, tell
Whom thou lovest best: see thou dissemble not.

BIAN. Believe me, sister, of all the men alive
I never yet beheld that special face
Which I could fancy more than any other.

KATH. Minion,[2] thou liest. Is 't not Hortensio?

BIAN. If you affect him, sister, here I swear
I 'll plead for you myself, but you shall have him.

KATH. O then, belike, you fancy riches more:
You will have Gremio to keep you fair.

BIAN. Is it for him you do envy me so?
Nay then you jest, and now I well perceive
You have but jested with me all this while:
I prithee, sister Kate, untie my hands.

KATH. If that be jest, then all the rest was so. [*Strikes her.*

[1] *for these other gawds*] as for these other toys, trifles.
[2] *Minion*] Saucy woman.

Enter BAPTISTA

BAP. Why, how now, dame! whence grows this insolence?
Bianca, stand aside. Poor girl! she weeps.
Go ply thy needle; meddle not with her.
For shame, thou hilding[3] of a devilish spirit,
Why dost thou wrong her that did ne'er wrong thee?
When did she cross thee with a bitter word?
KATH. Her silence flouts me, and I 'll be revenged.
[*Flies after Bianca.*
BAP. What, in my sight? Bianca, get thee in. [*Exit Bianca.*
KATH. What, will you not suffer me? Nay, now I see
She is your treasure, she must have a husband;
I must dance bare-foot[4] on her wedding day
And for your love to her lead apes in hell.[5]
Talk not to me: I will go sit and weep
Till I can find occasion of revenge. [*Exit.*
BAP. Was ever gentleman thus grieved as I?
But who comes here?

Enter GREMIO, LUCENTIO *in the habit of a mean man;* PETRUCHIO, *with* HORTENSIO *as a musician; and* TRANIO, *with* BIONDELLO *bearing a lute and books*

GRE. Good morrow, neighbour Baptista.
BAP. Good morrow, neighbour Gremio. God save you, gentlemen!
PET. And you, good sir; Pray, have you not a daughter
Call'd Katharina, fair and virtuous?
BAP. I have a daughter, sir, called Katharina.
GRE. You are too blunt: go to it orderly.
PET. You wrong me, Signior Gremio: give me leave.
I am a gentleman of Verona, sir,
That, hearing of her beauty and her wit,
Her affability and bashful modesty,

[3] *hilding*] base wretch, good-for-nothing.
[4] *dance barefoot*] it was a popular belief that an older, unmarried sister might prevent her own spinsterhood by dancing barefoot at her younger sister's wedding.
[5] *lead apes in hell*] the proverbial destiny of old maids and childless women.

Her wondrous qualities and mild behaviour,
Am bold to show myself a forward guest
Within your house, to make mine eye the witness
Of that report which I so oft have heard.
And, for an entrance to my entertainment,
I do present you with a man of mine, [*Presenting Hortensio.*
Cunning in music and the mathematics,
To instruct her fully in those sciences,
Whereof I know she is not ignorant:
Accept of him, or else you do me wrong:
His name is Licio, born in Mantua.

BAP. You 're welcome, sir; and he, for your good sake.
But for my daughter Katharine, this I know,
She is not for your turn, the more my grief.

PET. I see you do not mean to part with her,
Or else you like not of my company.

BAP. Mistake me not; I speak but as I find.
Whence are you, sir? what may I call your name?

PET. Petruchio is my name; Antonio's son,
A man well known throughout all Italy.

BAP. I know him well: you are welcome for his sake.

GRE. Saving your tale, Petruchio, I pray,
Let us, that are poor petitioners, speak too:
Baccare![6] you are marvellous forward.

PET. O, pardon me, Signior Gremio; I would fain be doing.

GRE. I doubt it not, sir; but you will curse your wooing.
Neighbour, this is a gift very grateful, I am sure of it. To express the like kindness, myself, that have been more kindly beholding to you than any, freely give unto you this young scholar [*presenting Lucentio*], that hath been long studying at Rheims; as cunning in Greek, Latin, and other languages, as the other in music and mathematics: his name is Cambio; pray, accept his service.

BAP. A thousand thanks, Signior Gremio. Welcome, good Cambio. But, gentle sir [*to Tranio*], methinks you walk like a stranger: may

6 *Baccare!*] A cant interjection meaning "get back."

I be so bold to know the cause of your coming?
TRA. Pardon me, sir, the boldness is mine own;
That, being a stranger in this city here,
Do make myself a suitor to your daughter,
Unto Bianca, fair and virtuous.
Nor is your firm resolve unknown to me,
In the preferment of the eldest sister.
This liberty is all that I request,
That, upon knowledge of my parentage,
I may have welcome 'mongst the rest that woo
And free access and favour as the rest:
And, toward the education of your daughters,
I here bestow a simple instrument,
And this small packet of Greek and Latin books:
If you accept them, then their worth is great.
BAP. Lucentio is your name; of whence, I pray?
TRA. Of Pisa, sir; son to Vincentio.
BAP. A mighty man of Pisa; by report
I know him well: you are very welcome, sir.
Take you the lute, and you the set of books;
You shall go see your pupils presently.
Holla, within!

Enter a Servant

Sirrah, lead these gentlemen
To my daughters; and tell them both,
These are their tutors: bid them use them well.
[*Exit Servant, with Luc. and Hor., Bio. following.*
We will go walk a little in the orchard,
And then to dinner. You are passing welcome,
And so I pray you all to think yourselves.
PET. Signior Baptista, my business asketh haste,
And every day I cannot come to woo.
You knew my father well, and in him me,
Left solely heir to all his lands and goods,
Which I have better'd rather than decreased:
Then tell me, if I get your daughter's love,

What dowry shall I have with her to wife?
BAP. After my death the one half of my lands,
And in possession twenty thousand crowns.
PET. And, for that dowry, I 'll assure her of
Her widowhood,[7] be it that she survive me,
In all my lands and leases whatsoever:
Let specialties[8] be therefore drawn between us,
That covenants may be kept on either hand.
BAP. Ay, when the special thing is well obtain'd,
That is, her love; for that is all in all.
PET. Why, that is nothing; for I tell you, father,
I am as peremptory as she proud-minded;
And where two raging fires meet together
They do consume the thing that feeds their fury:
Though little fire grows great with little wind,
Yet extreme gusts will blow out fire and all:
So I to her and so she yields to me;
For I am rough and woo not like a babe.
BAP. Well mayst thou woo, and happy be thy speed!
But be thou arm'd for some unhappy words.
PET. Ay, to the proof; as mountains are for winds,
That shake not, though they blow perpetually.

Re-enter HORTENSIO, *with his head broke*

BAP. How now, my friend! why dost thou look so pale?
HOR. For fear, I promise you, if I look pale.
BAP. What, will my daughter prove a good musician?
HOR. I think she 'll sooner prove a soldier:
Iron may hold with her, but never lutes.
BAP. Why, then thou canst not break her to the lute?
HOR. Why, no; for she hath broke the lute to me.
I did but tell her she mistook her frets,
And bow'd her hand to teach her fingering;
When, with a most impatient devilish spirit,

[7] *widowhood*] the dower or jointure of a widow.
[8] *specialties*] articles of a contract.

"Frets, call you these?" quoth she; "I 'll fume with them:"[9]
And, with that word, she struck me on the head,
And through the instrument my pate made way;
And there I stood amazed for a while,
As on a pillory, looking through the lute;
While she did call me rascal fiddler
And twangling Jack;[10] with twenty such vile terms,
As had she studied to misuse me so.

PET. Now, by the world, it is a lusty wench;
I love her ten times more than e'er I did:
O, how I long to have some chat with her!

BAP. Well, go with me and be not so discomfited:
Proceed in practice with my younger daughter;
She 's apt to learn and thankful for good turns.
Signior Petruchio, will you go with us,
Or shall I send my daughter Kate to you?

PET. I pray you do; I will attend her here,
[*Exeunt Baptista, Gremio, Tranio, and Hortensio.*
And woo her with some spirit when she comes.
Say that she rail; why then I 'll tell her plain
She sings as sweetly as a nightingale:
Say that she frown; I 'll say she looks as clear
As morning roses newly wash'd with dew:
Say she be mute and will not speak a word;
Then I 'll commend her volubility,
And say she uttereth piercing eloquence:
If she do bid me pack, I 'll give her thanks,
As though she bid me stay by her a week:
If she deny to wed, I 'll crave the day
When I shall ask the banns, and when be married.
But here she comes; and now, Petruchio, speak.

Enter KATHARINA

Good morrow, Kate; for that 's your name, I hear.

[9] *Frets . . . fume*] "To fret and fume" is a very common expression, meaning "to get angry."
[10] *twangling Jack*] strumming fool.

KATH. Well have you heard, but something hard of hearing:
They call me Katharine that do talk of me.
PET. You lie, in faith; for you are call'd plain Kate,
And bonny Kate, and sometimes Kate the curst;
But Kate, the prettiest Kate in Christendom,
Kate of Kate-Hall, my super-dainty Kate,
For dainties are all Kates,[11] and therefore, Kate,
Take this of me, Kate of my consolation;
Hearing thy mildness praised in every town,
Thy virtues spoke of, and thy beauty sounded,
Yet not so deeply as to thee belongs,
Myself am moved to woo thee for my wife.
KATH. Moved! in good time: let him that moved you hither
Remove you hence: I knew you at the first
You were a moveable.
PET. Why, what 's a moveable?
KATH. A join'd-stool.
PET. Thou hast hit it: come, sit on me.
KATH. Asses are made to bear, and so are you.
PET. Women are made to bear, and so are you.
KATH. No such jade as you, if me you mean.
PET. Alas, good Kate, I will not burden thee!
For, knowing thee to be but young and light, —
KATH. Too light for such a swain as you to catch;
And yet as heavy as my weight should be.
PET. Should be! should — buzz!
KATH. Well ta'en, and like a buzzard.
PET. O slow-wing'd turtle![12] shall a buzzard take thee?
KATH. Ay, for a turtle, as he takes a buzzard.
PET. Come, come, you wasp; i' faith, you are too angry.
KATH. If I be waspish, best beware my sting.
PET. My remedy is then, to pluck it out.
KATH. Ay, if the fool could find it where it lies.
PET. Who knows not where a wasp does wear his sting? In his tail.

[11] *For dainties are all Kates*] A quibble on "cates," confections.
[12] *turtle*] turtledove.

KATH. In his tongue.

PET. Whose tongue?

KATH. Yours, if you talk of tails: and so farewell.

PET. What, with my tongue in your tail? nay, come again,
Good Kate; I am a gentleman.

KATH. That I 'll try. [*She strikes him.*

PET. I swear I 'll cuff you, if you strike again.

KATH. So may you lose your arms:
If you strike me, you are no gentleman;
And if no gentleman, why then no arms.

PET. A herald, Kate? O, put me in thy books![13]

KATH. What is your crest? a coxcomb?

PET. A combless cock, so Kate will be my hen.

KATH. No cock of mine; you crow too like a craven.[14]

PET. Nay, come, Kate, come; you must not look so sour.

KATH. It is my fashion, when I see a crab.

PET. Why, here 's no crab; and therefore look not sour.

KATH. There is, there is.

PET. Then show it me.

KATH. Had I a glass, I would.

PET. What, you mean my face?

KATH. Well aim'd of such a young one.

PET. Now, by Saint George, I am too young for you.

KATH. Yet you are wither'd.

PET. 'T is with cares.

KATH. I care not.

PET. Nay, hear you, Kate: in sooth you scape not so.

KATH. I chafe you, if I tarry: let me go.

PET. No, not a whit: I find you passing gentle.
'T was told me you were rough and coy and sullen,
And now I find report a very liar;
For thou art pleasant, gamesome, passing courteous,
But slow in speech, yet sweet as spring-time flowers:

[13] *put me in thy books*] a quibble on the two senses of the phrase, viz., "taking one into favour" and "enrolling one's name in the registers (of the Herald's College)."

[14] *craven*] a worthless gamecock.

Thou canst not frown, thou canst not look askance,
Nor bite the lip, as angry wenches will,
Nor hast thou pleasure to be cross in talk,
But thou with mildness entertain'st thy wooers,
With gentle conference, soft and affable.
Why does the world report that Kate doth limp?
O slanderous world! Kate like the hazel-twig
Is straight and slender, and as brown in hue
As hazel-nuts and sweeter than the kernels.
O, let me see thee walk: thou dost not halt.

KATH. Go, fool, and whom thou keep'st command.

PET. Did ever Dian[15] so become a grove
As Kate this chamber with her princely gait?
O, be thou Dian, and let her be Kate;
And then let Kate be chaste and Dian sportful!

KATH. Where did you study all this goodly speech?

PET. It is extempore, from my mother-wit.

KATH. A witty mother! witless else her son.

PET. Am I not wise?

KATH. Yes; keep you warm.[16]

PET. Marry, so I mean, sweet Katharine, in thy bed:
And therefore, setting all this chat aside,
Thus in plain terms: your father hath consented
That you shall be my wife; your dowry 'greed on;
And, will you, nill you, I will marry you.
Now, Kate, I am a husband for your turn;
For, by this light, whereby I see thy beauty,
Thy beauty, that doth make me like thee well,
Thou must be married to no man but me;
For I am he am born to tame you Kate,
And bring you from a wild Kate to a Kate
Conformable as other household Kates.
Here comes your father: never make denial;

[15] *Dian*] goddess of chastity and the hunt.

[16] *keep you warm*] an allusion to some such proverbial phrase as "A wise man keeps out of the cold."

I must and will have Katharine to my wife.

Re-enter BAPTISTA, GREMIO, *and* TRANIO

BAP. Now, Signior Petruchio, how speed you with my daughter?
PET. How but well, sir? how but well?
It were impossible I should speed amiss.
BAP. Why, how now, daughter Katharine! in your dumps?
KATH. Call you me daughter? now, I promise you
You have show'd a tender fatherly regard,
To wish me wed to one half lunatic;
A mad-cap ruffian and a swearing Jack,
That thinks with oaths to face the matter out.
PET. Father, 't is thus: yourself and all the world,
That talk'd of her, have talk'd amiss of her:
If she be curst, it is for policy,
For she 's not froward, but modest as the dove;
She is not hot, but temperate as the morn;
For patience she will prove a second Grissel,
And Roman Lucrece[17] for her chastity:
And to conclude, we have 'greed so well together,
That upon Sunday is the wedding-day.
KATH. I 'll see thee hang'd on Sunday first.
GRE. Hark, Petruchio; she says she 'll see thee hang'd first.
TRA. Is this your speeding? nay, then, good night our part![18]
PET. Be patient, gentlemen; I choose her for myself:
If she and I be pleased, what 's that to you?
'T is bargain'd 'twixt us twain, being alone,
That she shall still be curst in company.
I tell you, 't is incredible to believe
How much she loves me: O, the kindest Kate!
She hung about my neck; and kiss on kiss
She vied so fast, protesting oath on oath,
That in a twink she won me to her love.

[17] *Grissel . . . Lucrece*] Griselda, the model of wifely patience, was the subject of works by Petrarch, Boccaccio and Chaucer; the chaste Lucrece, who took her life after her chastity had been violated, had her story told in Shakespeare's *Rape of Lucrece*.
[18] *our part*] our part of the bargain.

O, you are novices! 't is a world to see,[19]
How tame, when men and women are alone,
A meacock[20] wretch can make the curstest shrew.
Give me thy hand, Kate: I will unto Venice,
To buy apparel 'gainst the wedding-day.
Provide the feast, father, and bid the guests;
I will be sure my Katherine shall be fine.

BAP. I know not what to say: but give me your hands;
God send you joy, Petruchio! 't is a match.

GRE. TRA. Amen, say we: we will be witnesses.

PET. Father, and wife, and gentlemen, adieu
I will to Venice; Sunday comes apace:
We will have rings, and things, and fine array,
And, kiss me, Kate, we will be married o' Sunday.

[*Exeunt Petruchio and Katharina severally.*

GRE. Was ever match clapp'd up so suddenly?

BAP. Faith, gentlemen, now I play a merchant's part,
And venture madly on a desperate mart.

TRA. 'T was a commodity lay fretting by you:
'T will bring you gain, or perish on the seas.

BAP. The gain I seek is, quiet in the match.

GRE. No doubt but he hath got a quiet catch.[21]
But now, Baptista, to your younger daughter:
Now is the day we long have looked for:
I am your neighbour, and was suitor first.

TRA. And I am one that love Bianca more
Than words can witness, or your thoughts can guess.

GRE. Youngling, thou canst not love so dear as I.

TRA. Greybeard, thy love doth freeze.

GRE. But thine doth fry.
Skipper, stand back: 't is age that nourisheth.

TRA. But youth in ladies' eyes that flourisheth.

BAP. Content you, gentlemen: I will compound this strife:

[19] *a world to see*] a wonderful sight; a common Elizabethan expression.
[20] *meacock*] spiritless.
[21] *got a quiet catch*] made a safe haul.

'T is deeds must win the prize; and he, of both,
That can assure my daughter greatest dower
Shall have my Bianca's love.
Say, Signior Gremio, what can you assure her?
GRE. First, as you know, my house within the city
Is richly furnished with plate and gold;
Basins and ewers to lave her dainty hands;
My hangings all of Tyrian tapestry;
In ivory coffers I have stuff'd my crowns;
In cypress chests my arras counterpoints,
Costly apparel, tents, and canopies,[22]
Fine linen, Turkey cushions boss'd with pearl,
Valance of Venice gold in needlework,[23]
Pewter and brass and all things that belong
To house or housekeeping: then, at my farm
I have a hundred milch-kine to the pail,[24]
Sixscore fat oxen standing in my stalls,
And all things answerable to this portion.
Myself am struck in years, I must confess;
And if I die to-morrow, this is hers,
If whilst I live she will be only mine.
TRA. That "only" came well in. Sir, list to me:
I am my father's heir and only son:
If I may have your daughter to my wife,
I 'll leave her houses three or four as good,
Within rich Pisa walls, as any one
Old Signior Gremio has in Padua;
Besides two thousand ducats by the year
Of fruitful land, all which shall be her jointure.
What, have I pinch'd you,[25] Signior Gremio?
GRE. Two thousand ducats by the year of land!
My land amounts not to so much in all:
That she shall have; besides an argosy

[22] *tents, and canopies*] bed hangings.
[23] *Valance . . . needlework*] Drapery of the bedstead made of Venetian lace in gold thread.
[24] *milch-kine to the pail*] cows for milking.
[25] *pinch'd*] got the better of, hurt.

That now is lying in Marseilles' road.
What, have I choked you with an argosy?[26]

TRA. Gremio, 't is known my father hath no less
Than three great argosies; besides two galliasses,[27]
And twelve tight galleys: these I will assure her,
And twice as much, whate'er thou offer'st next.

GRE. Nay, I have offer'd all, I have no more;
And she can have no more than all I have:
If you like me, she shall have me and mine.

TRA. Why, then the maid is mine from all the world,
By your firm promise: Gremio is out-vied.

BAP. I must confess your offer is the best;
And, let your father make her the assurance,
She is your own; else, you must pardon me,
If you should die before him, where 's her dower?

TRA. That 's but a cavil: he is old, I young.

GRE. And may not young men die, as well as old?

BAP. Well, gentlemen,
I am thus resolved: on Sunday next you know
My daughter Katharine is to be married:
Now, on the Sunday following, shall Bianca
Be bride to you, if you make this assurance;[28]
If not, to Signior Gremio:
And so, I take my leave, and thank you both.

GRE. Adieu, good neighbour. [*Exit Baptista.*
Now I fear thee not:
Sirrah young gamester, your father were a fool
To give thee all, and in his waning age
Set foot under thy table: tut, a toy!
An old Italian fox is not so kind, my boy. [*Exit.*

TRA. A vengeance on your crafty wither'd hide!
Yet I have faced it with a card of ten.[29]

[26] *argosy*] the largest size of merchant vessel.
[27] *galliasses*] heavy, low-built merchant ships.
[28] *if . . . assurance*] if you give this security.
[29] *a card of ten*] a card of ten spots, which might, when skilfully played, count highest in "primero" and other contemporary games.

'T is in my head to do my master good:
I see no reason but supposed Lucentio
Must get a father, call'd — supposed Vincentio;
And that 's a wonder: fathers commonly
Do get their children; but in this case of wooing,
A child shall get a sire, if I fail not of my cunning. [*Exit.*

ACT III.

SCENE I. *Padua. Baptista's House.*

one week later, the wedding day

Enter LUCENTIO, HORTENSIO, *and* BIANCA

LUC. Fiddler, forbear; you grow too forward, sir:
Have you so soon forgot the entertainment
Her sister Katharine welcomed you withal?

HOR. But, wrangling pedant, this is
The patroness of heavenly harmony:
Then give me leave to have prerogative;
And when in music we have spent an hour,
Your lecture shall have leisure for as much.

LUC. Preposterous ass, that never read so far
To know the cause why music was ordain'd!
Was it not to refresh the mind of man
After his studies or his usual pain?[1]
Then give me leave to read philosophy,
And while I pause, serve in your harmony.

HOR. Sirrah, I will not bear these braves of thine.

BIAN. Why, gentlemen, you do me double wrong,
To strive for that which resteth in my choice:
I am no breeching scholar[2] in the schools;
I 'll not be tied to hours nor 'pointed times,
But learn my lessons as I please myself.
And, to cut off all strife, here sit we down:
Take you your instrument, play you the whiles;

[1] *his usual pain*] his customary toil.
[2] *breeching scholar*] a boy, fit to be breeched or flogged.

His lecture will be done ere you have tuned.

HOR. You 'll leave his lecture when I am in tune?

LUC. That will be never: tune your instrument.

BIAN. Where left we last?

LUC. Here, madam:

"Hic ibat Simois; hic est Sigeia tellus;
Hic steterat Priami regia celsa senis."[3]

BIAN. Construe them.

LUC. "Hic ibat," as I told you before, — "Simois," I am Lucentio, — "hic est," son unto Vincentio of Pisa, — "Sigeia tellus," disguised thus to get your love; — "Hic steterat," and that Lucentio that comes a-wooing, — "Priami," is my man Tranio, — "regia," bearing my port, — "celsa senis," that we might beguile the old pantaloon.

HOR. Madam, my instrument 's in tune.

BIAN. Let 's hear. O fie! the treble jars.

LUC. Spit in the hole, man, and tune again.

BIAN. Now let me see if I can construe it:
"Hic ibat Simois," I know you not, — "hic est Sigeia tellus," I trust you not, — "Hic steterat Priami," take heed he hear us not, — "regia," presume not, — "celsa senis," despair not.

HOR. Madam, 't is now in tune.

LUC. All but the base.

HOR. The base is right; 't is the base knave that jars.
[*Aside*] How fiery and forward our pedant is!
Now, for my life, the knave doth court my love:
Pedascule,[4] I 'll watch you better yet.

BIAN. In time I may believe, yet I mistrust.

LUC. Mistrust it not; for, sure, Æacides
Was Ajax, call'd so from his grandfather.

BIAN. I must believe my master; else, I promise you,
I should be arguing still upon that doubt:
But let it rest. Now, Licio, to you:

[3] *"Hic ibat . . . senis"*] "Here flowed the Simois; here is the Sigeian land; here stood the high palace of old Priam" (Ovid, *Heroides*, I, 33–34).

[4] *Pedascule*] Apparently a contemptuous diminutive of "pedant."

Good masters, take it not unkindly, pray,
That I have been thus pleasant with you both.

HOR. You may go walk, and give me leave a while:
My lessons make no music in three parts.

LUC. Are you so formal, sir? well, I must wait,
[*Aside*] And watch withal; for, but I be deceived,
Our fine musician groweth amorous.

HOR. Madam, before you touch the instrument,
To learn the order of my fingering,
I must begin with rudiments of art;
To teach you gamut[5] in a briefer sort,
More pleasant, pithy, and effectual,
Than hath been taught by any of my trade:
And there it is in writing, fairly drawn.

BIAN. Why, I am past my gamut long ago.

HOR. Yet read the gamut of Hortensio.

BIAN. [*reads*] " 'Gamut' I am, the ground of all accord,
'A re,' to plead Hortensio's passion;
'B mi,' Bianca, take him for thy lord,
'C fa ut,' that loves with all affection:
'D sol re,' one clef, two notes have I:
'E la mi,' show pity, or I die."

Call you this gamut? tut, I like it not:
Old fashions please me best; I am not so nice,
To change true rules for old inventions.

Enter a Servant

SERV. Mistress, your father prays you leave your books,
And help to dress your sister's chamber up:
You know to-morrow is the wedding-day.

BIAN. Farewell, sweet masters both; I must be gone.
[*Exeunt Bianca and Servant.*

LUC. Faith, mistress, then I have no cause to stay. [*Exit.*

HOR. But I have cause to pry into this pedant:
Methinks he looks as though he were in love:

[5] *gamut*] the scale in music.

Yet if thy thoughts, Bianca, be so humble,
To cast thy wandering eyes on every stale,
Seize thee that list: if once I find thee ranging,
Hortensio will be quit with thee by changing. [*Exit.*

SCENE II. *Padua. Before Baptista's House.*

Enter BAPTISTA, GREMIO, TRANIO, KATHARINA, BIANCA, LUCENTIO, *and* others, attendants

BAP. Signior Lucentio [*To Tranio*], this is the 'pointed day.
That Katharine and Petruchio should be married,
And yet we hear not of our son-in-law.
What will be said? what mockery will it be,
To want the bridegroom when the priest attends
To speak the ceremonial rites of marriage!
What says Lucentio to this shame of ours?
KATH. No shame but mine: I must, forsooth, be forced
To give my hand, opposed against my heart,
Unto a mad-brain rudesby, full of spleen;[1]
Who woo'd in haste, and means to wed at leisure.
I told you, I, he was a frantic fool,
Hiding his bitter jests in blunt behaviour:
And, to be noted for a merry man,
He 'll woo a thousand, 'point the day of marriage,
Make friends, invite, and proclaim the banns;
Yet never means to wed where he hath woo'd.
Now must the world point at poor Katharine,
And say, "Lo, there is mad Petruchio's wife,
If it would please him come and marry her!"
TRA. Patience, good Katharine, and Baptista too.
Upon my life, Petruchio means but well,

[1] *rudesby, full of spleen*] a ruffian, full of caprice, whimsical.

Whatever fortune stays him from his word:
Though he be blunt, I know him passing wise;
Though he be merry, yet withal he's honest.

KATH. Would Katharine had never seen him though!

[*Exit weeping, followed by Bianca and others.*

BAP. Go, girl; I cannot blame thee now to weep;
For such an injury would vex a very saint,
Much more a shrew of thy impatient humour.

Enter BIONDELLO

BION. Master, master! news, old news, and such news as you never heard of!

BAP. Is it new and old too? how may that be?

BION. Why, is it not news, to hear of Petruchio's coming?

BAP. Is he come?

BION. Why, no, sir.

BAP. What then?

BION. He is coming.

BAP. When will he be here?

BION. When he stands where I am and sees you there.

TRA. But say, what to thine old news?

BION. Why, Petruchio is coming in a new hat and an old jerkin, a pair of old breeches thrice turned, a pair of boots that have been candle-cases,[2] one buckled, another laced, an old rusty sword ta'en out of the town-armoury, with a broken hilt, and chapeless;[3] with two broken points: his horse hipped[4] with an old mothy saddle and stirrups of no kindred; besides, possessed with the glanders and like to mose in the chine; troubled with the lampass, infected with the fashions,[5] full of windgalls, sped with spavins, rayed with the yellows, past cure of the fives,[6] stark spoiled with the staggers, begnawn with the bots, swayed in the back and shoulder-shotten;

[2] *candle-cases*] used to keep candles in.

[3] *chapeless*] without the metal plate on the scabbard, especially at the point.

[4] *horse hipped*] This list of diseases in horses is conceived in a Rabelaisian vein.

[5] *fashions*] A corruption of the French word "farcin," a disease in horses.

[6] *fives*] "Fives," like "fashions," is a corruption of a French word. The disease, which is correctly known as "avives" or "vives," is an inflammation of the glands of the ear.

near-legged before and with a half-cheeked bit and a head-stall of sheep's leather which, being restrained to keep him from stumbling, hath been often burst and now repaired with knots; one girth six times pieced and a woman's crupper of velure, which hath two letters for her name fairly set down in studs, and here and there pieced with pack-thread.

BAP. Who comes with him?

BION. O, sir, his lackey, for all the world caparisoned like the horse; with a linen stock on one leg, and a kersey boot-hose on the other, gartered with a red and blue list; an old hat, and "the humour of forty fancies"[7] pricked in 't for a feather: a monster, a very monster in apparel, and not like a Christian footboy or a gentleman's lackey.

TRA. 'T is some odd humour pricks him to this fashion;
Yet oftentimes he goes but mean-apparell'd.

BAP. I am glad he 's come, howsoe'er he comes.

BION. Why, sir, he comes not.

BAP. Didst thou not say he comes?

BION. Who? that Petruchio came?

BAP. Ay, that Petruchio came.

BION. No, sir; I say his horse comes, with him on his back.

BAP. Why, that 's all one.

BION. Nay, by Saint Jamy,
I hold you a penny,
A horse and a man
Is more than one,
And yet not many.

Enter PETRUCHIO *and* GRUMIO

PET. Come, where be these gallants? who 's at home?

BAP. You are welcome, sir.

PET. And yet I come not well.

BAP. And yet you halt not.

TRA. Not so well apparell'd
As I wish you were.

[7] *"humour of forty fancies"*] possibly the title of a songbook or pamphlet.

PET. Were it better, I should rush in thus.
But where is Kate? where is my lovely bride?
How does my father? Gentles, methinks you frown:
And wherefore gaze this goodly company,
As if they saw some wondrous monument,
Some comet or unusual prodigy?
BAP. Why, sir, you know this is your wedding-day:
First were we sad, fearing you would not come;
Now sadder, that you come so unprovided.
Fie, doff this habit, shame to your estate,
An eye-sore to our solemn festival!
TRA. And tell us, what occasion of import
Hath all so long detain'd you from your wife,
And sent you hither so unlike yourself?
PET. Tedious it were to tell, and harsh to hear:
Sufficeth, I am come to keep my word,
Though in some part enforced to digress;
Which, at more leisure, I will so excuse
As you shall well be satisfied withal.
But where is Kate? I stay too long from her:
The morning wears, 't is time we were at church.
TRA. See not your bride in these unreverent robes:
Go to my chamber; put on clothes of mine.
PET. Not I, believe me: thus I 'll visit her.
BAP. But thus, I trust, you will not marry her.
PET. Good sooth, even thus; therefore ha' done with words:
To me she 's married, not unto my clothes:
Could I repair what she will wear in me,[8]
As I can change these poor accoutrements,
'T were well for Kate and better for myself.
But what a fool am I to chat with you,
When I should bid good morrow to my bride,
And seal the title with a lovely kiss!
[*Exeunt Petruchio and Grumio.*
TRA. He hath some meaning in his mad attire:

[8] *what . . . wear in me*] what she will wear out in me, what worry she will cause me.

We will persuade him, be it possible,
To put on better ere he go to church.
BAP. I 'll after him, and see the event of this.
[Exeunt Baptista, Gremio, and attendants.
TRA. But to her love concerneth us to add
Her father's liking: which to bring to pass,
As I before imparted to your worship,
I am to get a man, — whate'er he be,
It skills not much, we 'll fit him to our turn, —
And he shall be Vincentio of Pisa;
And make assurance here in Padua
Of greater sums than I have promised.
So shall you quietly enjoy your hope,
And marry sweet Bianca with consent.
LUC. Were it not that my fellow-schoolmaster
Doth watch Bianca's steps so narrowly,
'T were good, methinks, to steal our marriage;[9]
Which once perform'd, let all the world say no,
I 'll keep mine own, despite of all the world.
TRA. That by degrees we mean to look into,
And watch our vantage in this business:
We 'll over-reach the greybeard, Gremio,
The narrow-prying father, Minola,
The quaint musician, amorous Licio;
All for my master's sake, Lucentio.

Re-enter GREMIO

Signior Gremio, came you from the church?
GRE. As willingly as e'er I came from school.
TRA. And is the bride and bridegroom coming home?
GRE. A bridegroom say you? 't is a groom indeed,
A grumbling groom, and that the girl shall find.
TRA. Curster than she? why, 't is impossible.
GRE. Why, he 's a devil, a devil, a very fiend.
TRA. Why, she 's a devil, a devil, the devil's dam.

[9] *steal our marriage*] make our marriage clandestine.

GRE. Tut, she 's a lamb, a dove, a fool to him!
I 'll tell you, Sir Lucentio: when the priest
Should ask, if Katharine should be his wife,
"Ay, by gogs-wouns," quoth he; and swore so loud,
That, all amazed, the priest let fall the book;
And, as he stoop'd again to take it up,
This mad-brain'd bridegroom took him such a cuff,
That down fell priest and book, and book and priest:
"Now take them up," quoth he, "if any list."

TRA. What said the wench when he rose again?

GRE. Trembled and shook; for why he stamp'd and swore,
As if the vicar meant to cozen him.
But after many ceremonies done,
He calls for wine:[10] "A health!" quoth he; as if
He had been aboard, carousing to his mates
After a storm: quaff 'd off the muscadel,
And threw the sops all in the sexton's face;
Having no other reason
But that his beard grew thin and hungerly
And seem'd to ask him sops as he was drinking.
This done, he took the bride about the neck
And kiss'd her lips with such a clamorous smack
That at the parting all the church did echo:
And I seeing this came thence for very shame;
And after me, I know, the rout is coming.
Such a mad marriage never was before:
Hark, hark! I hear the minstrels play. [*Music.*

Re-enter PETRUCHIO, KATHARINA, BIANCA, BAPTISTA, HORTENSIO, GRUMIO, *and Train*

PET. Gentlemen and friends, I thank you for your pains:
I know you think to dine with me to-day,
And have prepared great store of wedding cheer;
But so it is, my haste doth call me hence,

[10] *He calls for wine*] It was the common practice to drink sweet wine, usually muscadel or muscadine, in church at the end of the wedding ceremony.

And therefore here I mean to take my leave.
BAP. Is 't possible you will away to-night?
PET. I must away to-day, before night come:
Make it no wonder; if you knew my business,
You would entreat me rather go than stay.
And, honest company, I thank you all,
That have beheld me give away myself
To this most patient, sweet, and virtuous wife:
Dine with my father, drink a health to me;
For I must hence; and farewell to you all.
TRA. Let us entreat you stay till after dinner.
PET. It may not be.
GRE. Let me entreat you.
PET. It cannot be.
KATH. Let me entreat you.
PET. I am content.
KATH. Are you content to stay?
PET. I am content you shall entreat me stay;
But yet not stay, entreat me how you can.
KATH. Now, if you love me, stay.
PET. Grumio, my horse.
GRU. Ay, sir, they be ready: the oats have eaten the horses.
KATH. Nay, then,
Do what thou canst, I will not go to-day;
No, nor to-morrow, not till I please myself.
The door is open, sir; there lies your way;
You may be jogging whiles your boots are green;[11]
For me, I 'll not be gone till I please myself:
'T is like you 'll prove a jolly surly groom,
That take it on you at the first so roundly.[12]
PET. O Kate, content thee; prithee, be not angry.
KATH. I will be angry: what hast thou to do?
Father, be quiet: he shall stay my leisure.
GRE. Ay, marry, sir, now it begins to work.

[11] *green*] fresh, new. The phrase might also be referring sarcastically to his attire.
[12] *That . . . roundly*] That at the outset behave so bluntly, so insolently.

KATH. Gentlemen, forward to the bridal dinner:
I see a woman may be made a fool,
If she had not a spirit to resist.

PET. They shall go forward, Kate, at thy command.
Obey the bride, you that attend on her;
Go to the feast, revel and domineer,
Carouse full measure to her maidenhead,
Be mad and merry, or go hang yourselves:
But for my bonny Kate, she must with me.
Nay, look not big, nor stamp, nor stare, nor fret;
I will be master of what is mine own:
She is my goods, my chattels; she is my house,
My household stuff, my field, my barn,
My horse, my ox, my ass, my any thing;
And here she stands, touch her whoever dare;
I 'll bring mine action on the proudest he
That stops my way in Padua. Grumio,
Draw forth thy weapon, we are beset with thieves;
Rescue thy mistress, if thou be a man.
Fear not, sweet wench, they shall not touch thee, Kate:
I 'll buckler thee against a million.
[*Exeunt Petruchio, Katharina, and Grumio.*

BAP. Nay, let them go, a couple of quiet ones.

GRE. Went they not quickly, I should die with laughing.

TRA. Of all mad matches never was the like.

LUC. Mistress, what 's your opinion of your sister?

BIAN. That, being mad herself, she 's madly mated.

GRE. I warrant him, Petruchio is Kated.

BAP. Neighbours and friends, though bride and bridegroom wants
For to supply the places at the table,
You know there wants no junkets at the feast.
Lucentio, you shall supply the bridegroom's place;
And let Bianca take her sister's room.

TRA. Shall sweet Bianca practise how to bride it?

BAP. She shall, Lucentio. Come, gentlemen, let 's go. [*Exeunt.*

ACT IV.

SCENE I. *Petruchio's Country House.*

Enter GRUMIO

GRU. Fie, fie on all tired jades, on all mad masters, and all foul ways! Was ever man so beaten? was ever man so rayed? was ever man so weary? I am sent before to make a fire, and they are coming after to warm them. Now, were not I a little pot, and soon hot, my very lips might freeze to my teeth, my tongue to the roof of my mouth, my heart in my belly, ere I should come by a fire to thaw me: but I, with blowing the fire, shall warm myself; for, considering the weather, a taller man than I will take cold. Holla, ho! Curtis!

Enter CURTIS

CURT. Who is it that calls so coldly?

GRU. A piece of ice: if thou doubt it, thou mayst slide from my shoulder to my heel with no greater a run but my head and my neck. A fire, good Curtis.

CURT. Is my master and his wife coming, Grumio?

GRU. O, ay, Curtis, ay: and therefore fire, fire; cast on no water.

CURT. Is she so hot a shrew as she 's reported?

GRU. She was, good Curtis, before this frost: but, thou knowest, winter tames man, woman, and beast; for it hath tamed my old master, and my new mistress, and myself, fellow Curtis.

CURT. Away, you three-inch fool![1] I am no beast.

[1] *three-inch fool*] a reference to Grumio's small stature.

GRU. Am I but three inches? why, thy horn is a foot; and so long am I at the least. But wilt thou make a fire, or shall I complain on thee to our mistress, whose hand, she being now at hand, thou shalt soon feel, to thy cold comfort, for being slow in thy hot office?

CURT. I prithee, good Grumio, tell me, how goes the world?

GRU. A cold world, Curtis, in every office but thine; and therefore fire: do thy duty, and have thy duty; for my master and mistress are almost frozen to death.

CURT. There 's fire ready; and therefore, good Grumio, the news.

GRU. Why, "Jack, boy! ho! boy!"[2] and as much news as thou wilt.

CURT. Come, you are so full of cony-catching!

GRU. Why, therefore fire; for I have caught extreme cold. Where 's the cook? is supper ready, the house trimmed, rushes strewed,[3] cobwebs swept; the serving-men in their new fustian, their white stockings, and every officer his wedding-garment on? Be the jacks fair within, the jills fair without, the carpets laid, and every thing in order?

CURT. All ready; and therefore, I pray thee, news.

GRU. First, know, my horse is tired; my master and mistress fallen out.

CURT. How?

GRU. Out of their saddles into the dirt; and thereby hangs a tale.

CURT. Let 's ha 't, good Grumio.

GRU. Lend thine ear.

CURT. Here.

GRU. There. [*Strikes him.*

CURT. This is to feel a tale, not to hear a tale.

GRU. And therefore 't is called a sensible tale: and this cuff was but to knock at your ear, and beseech listening. Now I begin: *Imprimis*,[4] we came down a foul hill, my master riding behind my mistress, —

CURT. Both of one horse?

GRU. What 's that to thee?

CURT. Why, a horse.

[2] *"Jack, boy! ho! boy!"*] The first words of an old round or catch.

[3] *rushes strewed*] The floors of Elizabethan houses were usually covered with rushes in place of carpets.

[4] *Imprimis*] In the first place.

GRU. Tell thou the tale: but hadst thou not crossed me, thou shouldst have heard how her horse fell and she under her horse; thou shouldst have heard in how miry a place, how she was bemoiled, how he left her with the horse upon her, how he beat me because her horse stumbled, how she waded through the dirt to pluck him off me, how he swore, how she prayed, that never prayed before, how I cried, how the horses ran away, how her bridle was burst, how I lost my crupper, with many things of worthy memory, which now shall die in oblivion and thou return unexperienced to thy grave.

CURT. By this reckoning he is more shrew than she.

GRU. Ay; and that thou and the proudest of you all shall find when he comes home. But what talk I of this? Call forth Nathaniel, Joseph, Nicholas, Philip, Walter, Sugarsop and the rest: let their heads be sleekly combed, their blue coats brushed, and their garters of an indifferent knit: let them curtsy with their left legs, and not presume to touch a hair of my master's horse-tail till they kiss their hands. Are they all ready?

CURT. They are.

GRU. Call them forth.

CURT. Do you hear, ho? you must meet my master to countenance my mistress!

GRU. Why, she hath a face of her own.

CURT. Who knows not that?

GRU. Thou, it seems, that calls for company to countenance[5] her.

CURT. I call them forth to credit her.

GRU. Why, she comes to borrow nothing of them.

Enter four or five serving-men

NATH. Welcome home, Grumio!

PHIL. How now, Grumio!

JOS. What, Grumio!

NICH. Fellow Grumio!

NATH. How now, old lad?

GRU. Welcome, you; — how now, you; — what, you; — fellow, you; —

[5] *countenance*] do grace or honour to.

and thus much for greeting. Now, my spruce companions, is all ready, and all things neat?

NATH. All things is ready. How near is our master?

GRU. E'en at hand, alighted by this; and therefore be not — Cock's passion, silence! I hear my master.

Enter PETRUCHIO *and* KATHARINA

PET. Where be these knaves? What, no man at door
To hold my stirrup nor to take my horse!
Where is Nathaniel, Gregory, Philip?

ALL SERV. Here, here, sir; here, sir.

PET. Here, sir! here, sir! here, sir! here sir!
You logger-headed and unpolish'd grooms!
What, no attendance? no regard? no duty?
Where is the foolish knave I sent before?

GRU. Here, sir; as foolish as I was before.

PET. You peasant swain! you whoreson malt-horse drudge!
Did I not bid thee meet me in the park,
And bring along these rascal knaves with thee?

GRU. Nathaniel's coat, sir, was not fully made,
And Gabriel's pumps were all unpink'd i' the heel;
There was no link to colour Peter's hat,
And Walter's dagger was not come from sheathing:
There were none fine but Adam, Ralph, and Gregory;
The rest were ragged, old, and beggarly;
Yet, as they are, here are they come to meet you.

PET. Go, rascals, go, and fetch my supper in. [*Exeunt servants.*

[*Singing*] Where is the life that late I led —

Where are those — Sit down, Kate, and welcome. —
Soud, soud, soud, soud![6]

Re-enter Servants *with supper*

Why, when, I say? Nay, good sweet Kate, be merry.
Off with my boots, you rogues! you villains, when?

[6] *Soud . . . soud*] An ejaculation expressive of fatigue.

[*Sings*] It was the friar of orders grey,
As he forth walked on his way: —

Out, you rogue! you pluck my foot awry:
Take that, and mend the plucking off the other. [*Strikes him.*
Be merry, Kate. Some water, here; what, ho!
Where 's my spaniel Troilus? Sirrah, get you hence,
And bid my cousin Ferdinand come hither:
One, Kate, that you must kiss, and be acquainted with.
Where are my slippers? Shall I have some water?

Enter one with water

Come, Kate, and wash, and welcome heartily.
You whoreson villain! will you let it fall? [*Strikes him.*
KATH. Patience, I pray you; 't was a fault unwilling.
PET. A whoreson beetle-headed, flap-ear'd knave!
Come, Kate, sit down; I know you have a stomach.
Will you give thanks, sweet Kate; or else shall I?
What 's this? mutton?
FIRST SERV. Ay.
PET. Who brought it?
PETER. I.
PET. 'T is burnt; and so is all the meat.
What dogs are these! where is the rascal cook?
How durst you, villains, bring it from the dresser,
And serve it thus to me that love it not?
There, take it to you, trenchers, cups, and all:
[*Throws the meat, &c. about the stage.*
You heedless joltheads and unmanner'd slaves!
What, do you grumble? I 'll be with you straight.
KATH. I pray you, husband, be not so disquiet:
The meat was well, if you were so contented.
PET. I tell thee, Kate, 't was burnt and dried away;
And I expressly am forbid to touch it,
For it engenders choler, planteth anger;
And better 't were that both of us did fast,
Since, of ourselves, ourselves are choleric,

Than feed it with such over-roasted flesh.
Be patient; to-morrow 't shall be mended,
And, for this night, we 'll fast for company:
Come, I will bring thee to thy bridal chamber. [*Exeunt.*

Re-enter Servants *severally*

NATH. Peter, didst ever see the like?
PETER. He kills her in her own humour.

Re-enter CURTIS

GRU. Where is he?
CURT. In her chamber, making a sermon of continency to her;
And rails, and swears, and rates, that she, poor soul,
Knows not which way to stand, to look, to speak,
And sits as one new-risen from a dream.
Away, away! for he is coming hither. [*Exeunt.*

Re-enter PETRUCHIO

PET. Thus have I politicly begun my reign,
And 't is my hope to end successfully.
My falcon[7] now is sharp and passing empty;
And till she stoop she must not be full-gorged,
For then she never looks upon her lure.
Another way I have to man my haggard,
To make her come and know her keeper's call,
That is, to watch her, as we watch these kites
That bate and beat and will not be obedient.
She eat no meat to-day, nor none shall eat;
Last night she slept not, nor to-night she shall not;
As with the meat, some undeserved fault
I 'll find about the making of the bed;
And here I 'll fling the pillow, there the bolster,
This way the coverlet, another way the sheets:

[7] *falcon*] This and the next six lines develop imagery derived from the sport of falconry. The full-fed hawk or falcon is not deceived by the "lure" or decoy made to look like a pigeon. A better way to master the "haggard" or wild falcon is to keep it awake or watchful, as is done with unruly kites that bate or flutter about and will not obey the falconer's call.

Ay, and amid this hurly I intend[8]
That all is done in reverend care of her;
And in conclusion she shall watch all night:
And if she chance to nod, I 'll rail and brawl,
And with the clamour keep her still awake.
This is a way to kill a wife with kindness;
And thus I 'll curb her mad and headstrong humour.
He that knows better how to tame a shrew,
Now let him speak: 't is charity to show. [*Exit.*

SCENE II. *Padua. Before Baptista's House.*

Enter TRANIO *and* HORTENSIO

TRA. Is 't possible, friend Licio, that Mistress Bianca
Doth fancy any other but Lucentio?
I tell you, sir, she bears me fair in hand.
HOR. Sir, to satisfy you in what I have said,
Stand by and mark the manner of his teaching.

Enter BIANCA *and* LUCENTIO

LUC. Now, mistress, profit you in what you read?
BIAN. What, master, read you? first resolve me that.
LUC. I read that I profess, the Art to Love.
BIAN. And may you prove, sir, master of your art!
LUC. While you, sweet dear, prove mistress of my heart!
HOR. Quick proceeders, marry! Now, tell me, I pray,
You that durst swear that your mistress Bianca
Loved none in the world so well as Lucentio.
TRA. O despiteful love! unconstant womankind!
I tell thee, Licio, this is wonderful.
HOR. Mistake no more: I am not Licio,

[8] *intend*] pretend.

Nor a musician, as I seem to be;
But one that scorn to live in this disguise,
For such a one as leaves a gentleman,
And makes a god of such a cullion:[1]
Know, sir, that I am call'd Hortensio.

TRA. Signior Hortensio, I have often heard
Of your entire affection to Bianca;
And since mine eyes are witness of her lightness,
I will with you, if you be so contented,
Forswear Bianca and her love for ever.

HOR. See, how they kiss and court! Signior Lucentio,
Here is my hand, and here I firmly vow
Never to woo her more, but do forswear her,
As one unworthy all the former favours
That I have fondly flatter'd her withal.

TRA. And here I take the like unfeigned oath,
Never to marry with her though she would entreat:
Fie on her! see, how beastly she doth court him!

HOR. Would all the world but he had quite forsworn!
For me, that I may surely keep mine oath,
I will be married to a wealthy widow,
Ere three days pass, which hath as long loved me
As I have loved this proud disdainful haggard.
And so farewell, Signior Lucentio.
Kindness in women, not their beauteous looks,
Shall win my love: and so I take my leave,
In resolution as I swore before. [*Exit.*

TRA. Mistress Bianca, bless you with such grace
As 'longeth to a lover's blessed case!
Nay, I have ta'en you napping, gentle love,
And have forsworn you with Hortensio.

BIAN. Tranio, you jest: but have you both forsworn me?

TRA. Mistress, we have.

LUC. Then we are rid of Licio.

[1] *cullion*] wretch.

TRA. I' faith, he 'll have a lusty widow now,
That shall be woo'd and wedded in a day.
BIAN. God give him joy!
TRA. Ay, and he 'll tame her.
BIAN. He says so, Tranio.
TRA. Faith, he is gone unto the taming-school.
BIAN. The taming-school! what, is there such a place?
TRA. Ay, mistress, and Petruchio is the master;
That teacheth tricks eleven and twenty long,[2]
To tame a shrew and charm her chattering tongue.

Enter BIONDELLO

BION. O master, master, I have watch'd so long
That I am dog-weary! but at last I spied
An ancient angel[3] coming down the hill,
Will serve the turn.
TRA. What is he, Biondello?
BION. Master, a mercatante,[4] or a pedant,
I know not what; but formal in apparel,
In gait and countenance surely like a father.
LUC. And what of him, Tranio?
TRA. If he be credulous and trust my tale,
I 'll make him glad to seem Vincentio,
And give assurance to Baptista Minola,
As if he were the right Vincentio.
Take in your love, and then let me alone.
[*Exeunt Lucentio and Bianca.*

Enter a Pedant

PED. God save you, sir!
TRA. And you, sir! you are welcome.
Travel you far on, or are you at the farthest?

[2] *tricks eleven and twenty long*] tricks of great intricacy or efficacy.
[3] *ancient angel*] metaphorically, a fellow of the old, good stamp, comparing the old coin stamped with an angel's image to the debased currency of the day.
[4] *mercatante*] merchant.

PED. Sir, at the farthest for a week or two:
But then up farther, and as far as Rome;
And so to Tripoli, if God lend me life.
TRA. What countryman, I pray?
PED. Of Mantua.
TRA. Of Mantua, sir? marry, God forbid!
And come to Padua, careless of your life?
PED. My life, sir! how, I pray? for that goes hard.
TRA. 'T is death for any one in Mantua
To come to Padua. Know you not the cause?
Your ships are stay'd at Venice; and the Duke,
For private quarrel 'twixt your duke and him,
Hath publish'd and proclaim'd it openly:
'T is marvel, but that you are but newly come,
You might have heard it else proclaim'd about.
PED. Alas, sir, it is worse for me than so!
For I have bills for money by exchange
From Florence, and must here deliver them.
TRA. Well, sir, to do you courtesy,
This will I do, and this I will advise you:
First, tell me, have you ever been at Pisa?
PED. Ay, sir, in Pisa have I often been;
Pisa renowned for grave citizens.
TRA. Among them know you one Vincentio?
PED. I know him not, but I have heard of him;
A merchant of incomparable wealth.
TRA. He is my father, sir; and, sooth to say,
In countenance somewhat doth resemble you.
BION. As much as an apple doth an oyster, and all one. [*Aside.*
TRA. To save your life in this extremity,
This favour will I do you for his sake;
And think it not the worst of all your fortunes
That you are like to Sir Vincentio.
His name and credit shall you undertake,
And in my house you shall be friendly lodged:
Look that you take upon you as you should;
You understand me, sir: so shall you stay

Till you have done your business in the city:
If this be courtesy, sir, accept of it.
PED. O sir, I do; and will repute you ever
The patron of my life and liberty.
TRA. Then go with me to make the matter good.
This, by the way, I let you understand;
My father is here look'd for every day,
To pass assurance of a dower in marriage
'Twixt me and one Baptista's daughter here:
In all these circumstances I 'll instruct you:
Go with me to clothe you as becomes you. [*Exeunt.*

SCENE III. ***A Room in Petruchio's House.***

Enter KATHARINA *and* GRUMIO

GRU. No, no, forsooth; I dare not for my life.
KATH. The more my wrong, the more his spite appears:
What, did he marry me to famish me?
Beggars, that come unto my father's door,
Upon entreaty have a present alms;
If not, elsewhere they meet with charity:
But I, who never knew how to entreat,
Nor never needed that I should entreat,
Am starved for meat, giddy for lack of sleep;
With oaths kept waking, and with brawling fed:
And that which spites me more than all these wants,
He does it under name of perfect love;
As who should say, if I should sleep or eat,
'T were deadly sickness or else present death.
I prithee go and get me some repast;
I care not what, so it be wholesome food.
GRU. What say you to a neat's[1] foot?

[1] *neat*] any cattle of the ox kind.

KATH. 'T is passing good: I prithee let me have it.
GRU. I fear it is too choleric a meat.
How say you to a fat tripe finely broil'd?
KATH. I like it well: good Grumio, fetch it me.
GRU. I cannot tell; I fear 't is choleric.
What say you to a piece of beef and mustard?
KATH. A dish that I do love to feed upon.
GRU. Ay, but the mustard is too hot a little.
KATH. Why then, the beef, and let the mustard rest.
GRU. Nay then, I will not: you shall have the mustard,
Or else you get no beef of Grumio.
KATH. Then both, or one, or any thing thou wilt.
GRU. Why then, the mustard without the beef.
KATH. Go, get thee gone, thou false deluding slave, [*Beats him.*
That feed'st me with the very name of meat:
Sorrow on thee and all the pack of you
That triumph thus upon my misery!
Go, get thee gone, I say.

Enter PETRUCHIO *and* HORTENSIO *with meat*

PET. How fares my Kate? What, sweeting, all amort?[2]
HOR. Mistress, what cheer?
KATH. Faith, as cold as can be.
PET. Pluck up thy spirits; look cheerfully upon me.
Here, love; thou see'st how diligent I am
To dress thy meat myself and bring it thee:
I am sure, sweet Kate, this kindness merits thanks.
What, not a word? Nay, then thou lovest it not;
And all my pains is sorted to no proof.[3]
Here, take away this dish.
KATH. I pray you, let it stand.
PET. The poorest service is repaid with thanks;
And so shall mine, before you touch the meat.
KATH. I thank you, sir.

[2] *all amort*] downcast, dispirited.
[3] *all . . . proof*] all my labour is to no purpose, has proved of no value.

HOR. Signior Petruchio, fie! you are to blame.
Come, Mistress Kate, I 'll bear you company.
PET. Eat it up all, Hortensio, if thou lovest me. [*Aside.*
Much good do it unto thy gentle heart!
Kate, eat apace: and now, my honey love,
Will we return unto thy father's house,
And revel it as bravely as the best,
With silken coats and caps and golden rings,
With ruffs and cuffs and fardingales and things;
With scarfs and fans and double change of bravery,
With amber bracelets, beads and all this knavery.
What, hast thou dined? The tailor stays thy leisure,
To deck thy body with his ruffling treasure.[4]

Enter Tailor

Come, tailor, let us see these ornaments;
Lay forth the gown.

Enter Haberdasher

What news with you, sir?
HAB. Here is the cap your worship did bespeak.
PET. Why, this was moulded on a porringer;
A velvet dish: fie, fie! 't is lewd and filthy:
Why, 't is a cockle or a walnut-shell,
A knack, a toy, a trick, a baby's cap:
Away with it! come, let me have a bigger.
KATH. I 'll have no bigger: this doth fit the time,
And gentlewomen wear such caps as these.
PET. When you are gentle, you shall have one too,
And not till then.
HOR. That will not be in haste. [*Aside.*
KATH. Why, sir, I trust I may have leave to speak;
And speak I will; I am no child, no babe:
Your betters have endured me say my mind,
And if you cannot, best you stop your ears.

[4] *ruffling treasure*] flaunting finery.

My tongue will tell the anger of my heart,
Or else my heart concealing it will break;
And rather than it shall, I will be free
Even to the uttermost, as I please, in words.

PET. Why, thou say'st true; it is a paltry cap,
A custard-coffin,[5] a bauble, a silken pie:
I love thee well, in that thou likest it not.

KATH. Love me or love me not, I like the cap;
And it I will have, or I will have none. [*Exit Haberdasher.*

PET. Thy gown? why, ay: come, tailor, let us see 't.
O mercy, God! what masquing stuff[6] is here?
What 's this? a sleeve? 't is like a demi-cannon:[7]
What, up and down, carved like an apple-tart?
Here 's snip and nip and cut and slish and slash,
Like to a censer[8] in a barber's shop:
Why, what, i' devil's name, tailor, call'st thou this?

HOR. I see she 's like to have neither cap nor gown. [*Aside.*

TAI. You bid me make it orderly and well,
According to the fashion and the time.

PET. Marry, and did; but if you be remember'd,
I did not bid you mar it to the time.
Go, hop me over every kennel home,
For you shall hop without my custom, sir:
I 'll none of it: hence! make your best of it.

KATH. I never saw a better-fashion'd gown,
More quaint, more pleasing, nor more commendable:
Belike you mean to make a puppet of me.

PET. Why, true; he means to make a puppet of thee.

TAI. She says your worship means to make a puppet of her.

PET. O monstrous arrogance! Thou liest, thou thread, thou thimble,
Thou yard, three-quarters, half-yard, quarter, nail!
Thou flea, thou nit, thou winter-cricket thou!

[5] *custard-coffin*] "Coffin" was the usual term for the paste covering a custard.
[6] *masquing stuff*] dress fitted for a masquerade.
[7] *demi-cannon*] a large gun, of about six and one-half inches' bore.
[8] *censer*] A brazier or fire-pan, in which sweet herbs were kept burning in a barber's shop. The cover was liberally perforated.

Braved in mine own house with a skein of thread?
Away, thou rag, thou quantity, thou remnant;
Or I shall so be-mete[9] thee with thy yard,
As thou shalt think on prating whilst thou livest!
I tell thee, I, that thou hast marr'd her gown.

TAI. Your worship is deceived; the gown is made
Just as my master had direction:
Grumio gave order how it should be done.

GRU. I gave him no order; I gave him the stuff.

TAI. But how did you desire it should be made?

GRU. Marry, sir, with needle and thread.

TAI. But did you not request to have it cut?

GRU. Thou hast faced[10] many things.

TAI. I have.

GRU. Face not me: thou hast braved many men; brave not me; I will neither be faced nor braved. I say unto thee, I bid thy master cut out the gown; but I did not bid him cut it to pieces: ergo, thou liest.

TAI. Why, here is the note of the fashion to testify.

PET. Read it.

GRU. The note lies in 's throat, if he say I said so.

TAI. [*reads*] "Imprimis, a loose-bodied gown:"

GRU. Master, if ever I said loose-bodied gown, sew me in the skirts of it, and beat me to death with a bottom of brown thread: I said a gown.

PET. Proceed.

TAI. [*reads*] "With a small compassed[11] cape:"

GRU. I confess the cape.

TAI. [*reads*] "With a trunk sleeve:"

GRU. I confess two sleeves.

TAI. [*reads*] "The sleeves curiously cut."

PET. Ay, there 's the villany.

GRU. Error i' the bill, sir; error i' the bill. I commanded the sleeves

[9] *be-mete*] measure.

[10] *faced*] trimmed with facings; with the quibbling implication of "confronted impudently" or "defied."

[11] *compassed*] circular.

should be cut out, and sewed up again; and that I 'll prove upon thee, though thy little finger be armed in a thimble.

TAI. This is true that I say: an I had thee in place where, thou shouldst know it.

GRU. I am for thee straight: take thou the bill, give me thy mete-yard, and spare not me.

HOR. God-a-mercy, Grumio! then he shall have no odds.

PET. Well, sir, in brief, the gown is not for me.

GRU. You are i' the right, sir: 't is for my mistress.

PET. Go, take it up unto thy master's use.

GRU. Villain, not for thy life: take up my mistress' gown for thy master's use!

PET. Why, sir, what's your conceit in that?

GRU. O, sir, the conceit is deeper than you think for:
Take up my mistress' gown to his master's use!
O, fie, fie, fie!

PET. Hortensio, say thou wilt see the tailor paid. [*Aside.*
Go take it hence; be gone, and say no more.

HOR. Tailor, I 'll pay thee for thy gown to-morrow:
Take no unkindness of his hasty words:
Away! I say; commend me to thy master. [*Exit Tailor.*

PET. Well, come, my Kate; we will unto your father's
Even in these honest mean habiliments:
Our purses shall be proud, our garments poor;
For 't is the mind that makes the body rich;
And as the sun breaks through the darkest clouds,
So honour peereth in the meanest habit.
What is the jay more precious than the lark,
Because his feathers are more beautiful?
Or is the adder better than the eel,
Because his painted skin contents the eye?
O, no, good Kate; neither art thou the worse
For this poor furniture and mean array.
If thou account'st it shame, lay it on me;
And therefore frolic: we will hence forthwith,
To feast and sport us at thy father's house.
Go, call my men, and let us straight to him;

And bring our horses unto Long-lane end;
There will we mount, and thither walk on foot.
Let 's see; I think 't is now some seven o'clock,
And well we may come there by dinner-time.
KATH. I dare assure you, sir, 't is almost two;
And 't will be supper-time ere you come there.
PET. It shall be seven ere I go to horse:
Look, what I speak, or do, or think to do,
You are still crossing it. Sirs, let 't alone:
I will not go to-day; and ere I do,
It shall be what o'clock I say it is.
HOR. Why, so this gallant will command the sun. [*Exeunt.*

SCENE IV. *Padua. Before Baptista's House.*

Enter TRANIO, *and the* Pedant *dressed like* VINCENTIO

TRA. Sir, this is the house: please it you that I call?
PED. Ay, what else? and but I be deceived
Signior Baptista may remember me,
Near twenty years ago, in Genoa,
Where we were lodgers at the Pegasus.[1]
TRA. 'T is well; and hold your own, in any case,
With such austerity as 'longeth to a father.
PED. I warrant you.

Enter BIONDELLO

But, sir, here comes your boy;
'T were good he were school'd.
TRA. Fear you not him. Sirrah Biondello,
Now do your duty throughly, I advise you:
Imagine 't were the right Vincentio.
BION. Tut, fear not me.
TRA. But hast thou done thy errand to Baptista?

[1] *Pegasus*] an inn.

BION. I told him that your father was at Venice;
And that you look'd for him this day in Padua.
TRA. Thou 'rt a tall fellow: hold thee that to drink.
Here comes Baptista: set your countenance, sir.

Enter BAPTISTA *and* LUCENTIO

Signior Baptista, you are happily met.
[*To the Pedant*] Sir, this is the gentleman I told you of:
I pray you, stand good father to me now,
Give me Bianca for my patrimony.
PED. Soft, son!
Sir, by your leave: having come to Padua
To gather in some debts, my son Lucentio
Made me acquainted with a weighty cause
Of love between your daughter and himself:
And, for the good report I hear of you,
And for the love he beareth to your daughter,
And she to him, to stay him not too long,
I am content, in a good father's care,
To have him match'd; and, if you please to like
No worse than I, upon some agreement
Me shall you find ready and willing
With one consent to have her so bestow'd;
For curious I cannot be with you,
Signior Baptista, of whom I hear so well.
BAP. Sir, pardon me in what I have to say:
Your plainness and your shortness please me well.
Right true it is, your son Lucentio here
Doth love my daughter, and she loveth him,
Or both dissemble deeply their affections:
And therefore, if you say no more than this,
That like a father you will deal with him,
And pass[2] my daughter a sufficient dower,
The match is made, and all is done:
Your son shall have my daughter with consent.

[2] *pass*] make conveyance to.

TRA. I thank you, sir. Where then do you know best
We be affied[3] and such assurance ta'en
As shall with either part's agreement stand?
BAP. Not in my house, Lucentio; for, you know,
Pitchers have ears, and I have many servants:
Besides, old Gremio is hearkening still;
And happily[4] we might be interrupted.
TRA. Then at my lodging, an it like you:
There doth my father lie; and there, this night,
We 'll pass the business privately and well.
Send for your daughter by your servant here;
My boy shall fetch the scrivener presently.
The worst is this, that, at so slender warning,
You are like to have a thin and slender pittance.
BAP. It likes me well. Cambio, hie you home,
And bid Bianca make her ready straight;
And, if you will, tell what hath happened,
Lucentio's father is arrived in Padua,
And how she 's like to be Lucentio's wife.
BION. I pray the gods she may with all my heart!
TRA. Dally not with the gods, but get thee gone. [*Exit Bion.*
Signior Baptista, shall I lead the way?
Welcome! one mess is like to be your cheer:
Come, sir; we will better it in Pisa.
BAP. I follow you. [*Exeunt Tranio, Pedant, and Baptista.*

Re-enter BIONDELLO

BION. Cambio.
LUC. What sayest thou, Biondello?
BION. You saw my master wink and laugh upon you?
LUC. Biondello, what of that?
BION. Faith, nothing; but has left me here behind, to expound the meaning or moral of his signs and tokens.
LUC. I pray thee, moralize them.

[3] *affied*] betrothed.
[4] *happily*] haply, perhaps.

BION. Then thus. Baptista is safe, talking with the deceiving father of a deceitful son.

LUC. And what of him?

BION. His daughter is to be brought by you to the supper.

LUC. And then?

BION. The old priest at Saint Luke's church is at your command at all hours.

LUC. And what of all this?

BION. I cannot tell; expect they are busied about a counterfeit assurance: take you assurance of her, "cum privilegio ad imprimendum solum:"[5] to the church; take the priest, clerk, and some sufficient honest witnesses:
If this be not that you look for, I have no more to say,
But bid Bianca farewell for ever and a day.

LUC. Hearest thou, Biondello?

BION. I cannot tarry: I knew a wench married in an afternoon as she went to the garden for parsley to stuff a rabbit; and so may you, sir: and so, adieu, sir. My master hath appointed me to go to Saint Luke's, to bid the priest be ready to come against you come with your appendix. [*Exit.*

LUC. I may, and will, if she be so contented:
She will be pleased; then wherefore should I doubt?
Hap what hap may, I 'll roundly go about her:[6]
It shall go hard if Cambio go without her. [*Exit.*

SCENE V. A *Public Road.*

Enter PETRUCHIO, KATHARINA, HORTENSIO *and* Servants

PET. Come on, i' God's name; once more toward our father's.
Good Lord, how bright and goodly shines the moon!

KATH. The moon! the sun: it is not moonlight now.

[5] *cum privilegio, etc.*] with exclusive copyright.
[6] *I 'll roundly . . . her*] I 'll be blunt or outspoken with her.

PET. I say it is the moon that shines so bright.
KATH. I know it is the sun that shines so bright.
PET. Now, by my mother's son, and that 's myself,
It shall be moon, or star, or what I list,
Or ere I journey to your father's house.
Go on, and fetch our horses back again.
Evermore cross'd and cross'd; nothing but cross'd!
HOR. Say as he says, or we shall never go.
KATH. Forward, I pray, since we have come so far,
And be it moon, or sun, or what you please:
And if you please to call it a rush-candle,
Henceforth I vow it shall be so for me.
PET. I say it is the moon.
KATH. I know it is the moon.
PET. Nay, then you lie: it is the blessed sun.
KATH. Then, God be bless'd, it is the blessed sun:
But sun it is not, when you say it is not;
And the moon changes even as your mind.
What you will have it named, even that it is;
And so it shall be so for Katharine.
HOR. Petruchio, go thy ways; the field is won.
PET. Well, forward, forward! thus the bowl should run,
And not unluckily against the bias.[1]
But, soft! company is coming here.

Enter VINCENTIO

[*To Vincentio*] Good morrow, gentle mistress: where away?
Tell me, sweet Kate, and tell me truly too,
Hast thou beheld a fresher gentlewoman?
Such war of white and red within her cheeks!
What stars do spangle heaven with such beauty,
As those two eyes become that heavenly face?
Fair lovely maid, once more good day to thee.
Sweet Kate, embrace her for her beauty's sake.
HOR. A' will make the man mad, to make a woman of him.

[1] *against the bias*] contrary to tendency or propensity, a technical term in the game of bowls.

KATH. Young budding virgin, fair and fresh and sweet,
Whither away, or where is thy abode?
Happy the parents of so fair a child;
Happier the man, whom favourable stars
Allot thee for his lovely bed-fellow!
PET. Why, how now, Kate! I hope thou art not mad:
This is a man, old, wrinkled, faded, wither'd;
And not a maiden, as thou say'st he is.
KATH. Pardon, old father, my mistaking eyes,
That have been so bedazzled with the sun,
That every thing I look on seemeth green:
Now I perceive thou art a reverend father;
Pardon, I pray thee, for my mad mistaking.
PET. Do, good old grandsire; and withal make known
Which way thou travellest: if along with us,
We shall be joyful of thy company.
VIN. Fair sir, and you my merry mistress,
That with your strange encounter much amazed me,
My name is call'd Vincentio; my dwelling Pisa;
And bound I am to Padua; there to visit
A son of mine, which long I have not seen.
PET. What is his name?
VIN. Lucentio, gentle sir.
PET. Happily met; the happier for thy son.
And now by law, as well as reverend age,
I may entitle thee my loving father:
The sister to my wife, this gentlewoman,
Thy son by this hath married. Wonder not,
Nor be not grieved: she is of good esteem,
Her dowry wealthy, and of worthy birth;
Beside, so qualified as may beseem
The spouse of any noble gentleman.
Let me embrace with old Vincentio,
And wander we to see thy honest son,
Who will of thy arrival be full joyous.
VIN. But is this true? or is it else your pleasure,
Like pleasant travellers, to break a jest

Upon the company you overtake?

HOR. I do assure thee, father, so it is.

PET. Come, go along, and see the truth hereof;
For our first merriment hath made thee jealous.

[*Exeunt all but Hortensio.*

HOR. Well, Petruchio, this has put me in heart.
Have to my widow! and if she be froward,
Then hast thou taught Hortensio to be untoward. [*Exit.*

ACT V.

SCENE I. *Padua. Before Lucentio's House.*

GREMIO *discovered. Enter behind* BIONDELLO, LUCENTIO, *and* BIANCA

BION. Softly and swiftly, sir; for the priest is ready.

LUC. I fly, Biondello: but they may chance to need thee at home; therefore leave us.

BION. Nay, faith, I 'll see the church o' your back; and then come back to my master's as soon as I can.

[*Exeunt Lucentio, Bianca, and Biondello.*

GRE. I marvel Cambio comes not all this while.

Enter PETRUCHIO, KATHARINA, VINCENTIO, GRUMIO, *with* Attendants

PET. Sir, here 's the door, this is Lucentio's house:
My father's bears more toward the market-place;
Thither must I, and here I leave you, sir.

VIN. You shall not choose but drink before you go:
I think I shall command your welcome here,
And, by all likelihood, some cheer is toward. [*Knocks.*

GRE. They 're busy within; you were best knock louder.

Pedant *looks out of the window*

PED. What 's he that knocks as he would beat down the gate?

VIN. Is Signior Lucentio within, sir?

PED. He 's within, sir, but not to be spoken withal.

VIN. What if a man bring him a hundred pound or two, to make merry withal?

PED. Keep your hundred pounds to yourself: he shall need none, so long as I live.

PET. Nay, I told you your son was well beloved in Padua. Do you hear, sir? — to leave frivolous circumstances, — I pray you, tell Signior Lucentio, that his father is come from Pisa, and is here at the door to speak with him.

PED. Thou liest: his father has come from Padua, and here looking out at the window.

VIN. Art thou his father?

PED. Ay, sir; so his mother says, if I may believe her.

PET. [*To Vincentio*] Why, how now, gentleman! why, this is flat knavery, to take upon you another man's name.

PED. Lay hands on the villain: I believe a' means to cozen somebody in this city under my countenance.

Re-enter BIONDELLO

BION. I have seen them in the church together: God send 'em good shipping! But who is here? mine old master Vincentio! now we are undone, and brought to nothing.

VIN. [*Seeing Biondello*] Come hither, crack-hemp.[1]

BION. I hope I may choose, sir.[2]

VIN. Come hither, you rogue. What, have you forgot me?

BION. Forgot you! no, sir: I could not forget you, for I never saw you before in all my life.

VIN. What, you notorious villain, didst thou never see thy master's father, Vincentio?

BION. What, my old worshipful old master? yes, marry, sir: see where he looks out of the window.

VIN. Is 't so, indeed? [*Beats Biondello.*

BION. Help, help, help! here 's a madman will murder me. [*Exit.*

PED. Help, son! help, Signior Baptista! [*Exit from above.*

PET. Prithee, Kate, let 's stand aside, and see the end of this controversy. [*They retire.*

Re-enter Pedant *below;* TRANIO, BAPTISTA, *and* Servants

TRA. Sir, what are you, that offer to beat my servant?

[1] *crack-hemp*] a rogue that deserves to be hanged.
[2] *I hope . . . sir*] Allow me to decide that myself, sir.

VIN. What am I, sir! nay, what are you, sir? O immortal gods! O fine villain! A silken doublet! a velvet hose! a scarlet cloak! and a copatain hat![3] O, I am undone! I am undone! while I play the good husband at home, my son and my servant spend all at the university.

TRA. How now! what's the matter?

BAP. What, is the man lunatic?

TRA. Sir, you seem a sober ancient gentleman by your habit, but your words show you a madman. Why, sir, what 'cerns it you if I wear pearl and gold? I thank my good father, I am able to maintain it.

VIN. Thy father! O villain! he is a sail-maker in Bergamo.

BAP. You mistake, sir, you mistake, sir. Pray, what do you think is his name?

VIN. His name! as if I knew not his name: I have brought him up ever since he was three years old, and his name is Tranio.

PED. Away, away, mad ass! his name is Lucentio; and he is mine only son, and heir to the lands of me, Signior Vincentio.

VIN. Lucentio! O, he hath murdered his master! Lay hold on him, I charge you, in the Duke's name. O, my son, my son! Tell me, thou villain, where is my son Lucentio?

TRA. Call forth an officer.

Enter one with an Officer

Carry this mad knave to the gaol. Father Baptista, I charge you see that he be forthcoming.

VIN. Carry me to the gaol!

GRE. Stay, officer: he shall not go to prison.

BAP. Talk not, Signior Gremio: I say he shall go to prison.

GRE. Take heed, Signior Baptista, lest you be cony-catched in this business: I dare swear this is the right Vincentio.

PED. Swear, if thou darest.

GRE. Nay, I dare not swear it.

TRA. Then thou wert best say that I am not Lucentio.

GRE. Yes, I know thee to be Signior Lucentio.

[3] *copatain hat*] a hat with a high crown in the form of a sugar-loaf.

BAP. Away with the dotard! to the gaol with him!
VIN. Thus strangers may be haled and abused:
O monstrous villain!

Re-enter BIONDELLO, *with* LUCENTIO *and* BIANCA

BION. O, we are spoiled! and — yonder he is: deny him, forswear him, or else we are all undone.
LUC. Pardon, sweet father. [*Kneeling.*
VIN. Lives my sweet son?
[*Exeunt Biondello, Tranio, and Pedant, as fast as may be.*
BIAN. Pardon, dear father.
BAP. How hast thou offended?
Where is Lucentio?
LUC. Here's Lucentio,
Right son to the right Vincentio;
That have by marriage made thy daughter mine,
While counterfeit supposes[4] blear'd thine eyne.
GRE. Here 's packing, with a witness,[5] to deceive us all!
VIN. Where is that damned villain Tranio,
That faced and braved me in this matter so?
BAP. Why, tell me, is not this my Cambio?
BIAN. Cambio is changed into Lucentio.
LUC. Love wrought these miracles. Bianca's love
Made me exchange my state with Tranio,
While he did bear my countenance in the town;
And happily I have arrived at the last
Unto the wished haven of my bliss.
What Tranio did, myself enforced him to;
Then pardon him, sweet father, for my sake.
VIN. I 'll slit the villain's nose, that would have sent me to the gaol.
BAP. But do you hear, sir? have you married my daughter without asking my good will?
VIN. Fear not, Baptista; we will content you, go to: but I will in, to be revenged for this villany. [*Exit.*

[4] *counterfeit supposes*] false assumptions or suppositions.
[5] *Here 's packing, with a witness*] Here 's a gross piece of plotting, of a surety; here 's trickery, beyond all question.

BAP. And I, to sound the depth of this knavery. [*Exit.*
LUC. Look not pale, Bianca; thy father will not frown.
[*Exeunt Lucentio and Bianca.*
GRE. My cake is dough: but I 'll in among the rest;
Out of hope of all, but my share of the feast. [*Exit.*
KATH. Husband, let 's follow, to see the end of this ado.
PET. First kiss me, Kate, and we will.
KATH. What, in the midst of the street?
PET. What, art thou ashamed of me?
KATH. No, sir, God forbid; but ashamed to kiss.
PET. Why, then let 's home again. Come, sirrah, let 's away.
KATH. Nay, I will give thee a kiss: now pray thee, love, stay.
PET. Is not this well? Come, my sweet Kate:
Better once than never, for never too late. [*Exeunt.*

SCENE II. *Padua. Lucentio's House.*

Enter BAPTISTA, VINCENTIO, GREMIO, *the* Pedant, LUCENTIO, BIANCA, PETRUCHIO, KATHARINA, HORTENSIO, *and* Widow, TRANIO, BIONDELLO, *and* GRUMIO: *the Serving-men with Tranio bringing in a banquet.*

LUC. At last, though long, our jarring notes agree:
And time it is, when raging war is done,
To smile at scapes and perils overblown.
My fair Bianca, bid my father welcome,
While I with self-same kindness welcome thine.
Brother Petruchio, sister Katharina,
And thou, Hortensio, with thy loving widow,
Feast with the best, and welcome to my house:
My banquet[1] is to close our stomachs up,
After our great good cheer. Pray you, sit down;
For now we sit to chat, as well as eat.
PET. Nothing but sit and sit, and eat and eat!

[1] *banquet*] dessert.

BAP. Padua affords this kindness, son Petruchio.
PET. Padua affords nothing but what is kind.
HOR. For both our sakes, I would that word were true.
PET. Now, for my life, Hortensio fears his widow.
WID. Then never trust me, if I be afeard.[2]
PET. You are very sensible, and yet you miss my sense:
I mean, Hortensio is afeard of you.
WID. He that is giddy thinks the world turns round.
PET. Roundly replied.
KATH. Mistress, how mean you that?
WID. Thus I conceive by him.
PET. Conceives by me! How likes Hortensio that?
HOR. My widow says, thus she conceives her tale.
PET. Very well mended. Kiss him for that, good widow.
KATH. "He that is giddy thinks the world turns round:"
I pray you, tell me what you meant by that.
WID. Your husband, being troubled with a shrew,
Measures my husband's sorrow by his woe:
And now you know my meaning.
KATH. A very mean meaning.
WID. Right, I mean you.
KATH. And I am mean, indeed, respecting you.
PET. To her, Kate!
HOR. To her, widow!
PET. A hundred marks, my Kate does put her down.
HOR. That 's my office.
PET. Spoke like an officer: ha' to thee, lad. [*Drinks to Hortensio.*
BAP. How likes Gremio these quick-witted folks?
GRE. Believe me, sir, they butt together well.
BIAN. Head, and butt! an hasty-witted body
Would say your head and butt were head and horn.
VIN. Ay, mistress bride, hath that awaken'd you?
BIAN. Ay, but not frighted me; therefore I 'll sleep again.
PET. Nay, that you shall not: since you have begun,

[2] *fears . . . afeard*] The widow understands Petruchio to use the word "fears" in the causative sense of "frightens," instead of in the normal passive sense of "dreads."

Have at you for a bitter jest or two!
BIAN. Am I your bird? I mean to shift my bush;
And then pursue me as you draw your bow.
You are welcome all. [*Exeunt Bianca, Katharina, and Widow.*
PET. She hath prevented me. Here, Signior Tranio,
This bird you aim'd at, though you hit her not;
Therefore a health to all that shot and miss'd.
TRA. O, sir, Lucentio slipp'd me like his greyhound,
Which runs himself, and catches for his master.
PET. A good swift simile, but something currish.
TRA. 'T is well, sir, that you hunted for yourself:
'T is thought your deer does hold you at a bay.
BAP. O ho, Petruchio! Tranio hits you now.
LUC. I thank thee for that gird, good Tranio.
HOR. Confess, confess, hath he not hit you here?
PET. A' has a little gall'd me, I confess;
And, as the jest did glance away from me,
'T is ten to one it maim'd you two outright.
BAP. Now, in good sadness,[3] son Petruchio,
I think thou hast the veriest shrew of all.
PET. Well, I say no: and therefore for assurance
Let 's each one send unto his wife;
And he whose wife is most obedient,
To come at first when he doth send for her,
Shall win the wager which we will propose.
HOR. Content. What is the wager?
LUC. Twenty crowns.
PET. Twenty crowns!
I 'll venture so much of my hawk or hound,
But twenty times so much upon my wife.
LUC. A hundred then.
HOR. Content.
PET. A match! 't is done.
HOR. Who shall begin?
LUC. That will I.

[3] *in good sadness*] in sober earnest.

Go, Biondello, bid your mistress come to me.
BION. I go. [*Exit.*
BAP. Son, I 'll be your half, Bianca comes.
LUC. I 'll have no halves; I 'll bear it all myself.

Re-enter BIONDELLO

How now! what news?
BION. Sir, my mistress sends you word
That she is busy, and she cannot come.
PET. How! she is busy, and she cannot come!
Is that an answer?
GRE. Ay, and a kind one too:
Pray God, sir, your wife send you not a worse.
PET. I hope, better.
HOR. Sirrah Biondello, go and entreat my wife
To come to me forthwith. [*Exit Biondello.*
PET. O, ho! entreat her!
Nay, then she must needs come.
HOR. I am afraid, sir,
Do what you can, yours will not be entreated.

Re-enter BIONDELLO

Now, where 's my wife?
BION. She says you have some goodly jest in hand:
She will not come; she bids you come to her.
PET. Worse and worse; she will not come! O vile,
Intolerable, not to be endured!
Sirrah Grumio, go to your mistress;
Say, I command her come to me. [*Exit Grumio.*
HOR. I know her answer.
PET. What?
HOR. She will not.
PET. The fouler fortune mine, and there an end.
BAP. Now, by my holidame,[4] here comes Katharina!

[4] *holidame*] halidom.

Re-enter KATHARINA

KATH. What is your will, sir, that you send for me?
PET. Where is your sister, and Hortensio's wife?
KATH. They sit conferring by the parlour fire.
PET. Go, fetch them hither: if they deny to come,
Swinge[5] me them soundly forth unto their husbands:
Away, I say, and bring them hither straight. [*Exit Katharina.*
LUC. Here is a wonder, if you talk of a wonder.
HOR. And so it is: I wonder what it bodes.
PET. Marry, peace it bodes, and love, and quiet life,
An awful[6] rule, and right supremacy;
And, to be short, what not, that 's sweet and happy?
BAP. Now, fair befal thee, good Petruchio!
The wager thou hast won; and I will add
Unto their losses twenty thousand crowns;
Another dowry to another daughter,
For she is changed, as she had never been.
PET. Nay, I will win my wager better yet,
And show more sign of her obedience,
Her new-built virtue and obedience.
See where she comes and brings your froward wives
As prisoners to her womanly persuasion.

Re-enter KATHARINA, *with* BIANCA *and* Widow

Katharine, that cap of yours becomes you not:
Off with that bauble, throw it under-foot.
WID. Lord, let me never have a cause to sigh,
Till I be brought to such a silly pass!
BIAN. Fie, what a foolish duty call you this?
LUC. I would your duty were as foolish too:
The wisdom of your duty, fair Bianca,
Hath cost me an hundred crowns since supper-time.
BIAN. The more fool you, for laying on my duty.
PET. Katharine, I charge thee, tell these headstrong women

[5] *swinge*] thrash.
[6] *awful*] inspiring awe.

What duty they do owe their lords and husbands.
WID. Come, come, you 're mocking: we will have no telling.
PET. Come on, I say; and first begin with her.
WID. She shall not.
PET. I say she shall: and first begin with her.
KATH. Fie, fie! unknit that threatening unkind brow;
And dart not scornful glances from those eyes,
To wound thy lord, thy king, thy governor:
It blots thy beauty as frosts do bite the meads,
Confounds thy fame as whirlwinds shake fair buds,
And in no sense is meet or amiable.
A woman moved is like a fountain troubled,
Muddy, ill-seeming, thick, bereft of beauty;
And while it is so, none so dry or thirsty
Will deign to sip or touch one drop of it.
Thy husband is thy lord, thy life, thy keeper,
Thy head, thy sovereign; one that cares for thee,
And for thy maintenance commits his body
To painful labour both by sea and land,
To watch the night in storms, the day in cold,
Whilst thou liest warm at home, secure and safe;
And craves no other tribute at thy hands
But love, fair looks and true obedience;
Too little payment for so great a debt.
Such duty as the subject owes the prince
Even such a woman oweth to her husband;
And when she is froward, peevish, sullen, sour,
And not obedient to his honest will,
What is she but a foul contending rebel,
And graceless traitor to her loving lord?
I am ashamed that women are so simple
To offer war where they should kneel for peace;
Or seek for rule, supremacy and sway,
When they are bound to serve, love and obey.
Why are our bodies soft and weak and smooth,
Unapt to toil and trouble in the world,

But that our soft conditions[7] and our hearts
Should well agree with our external parts?
Come, come, you froward and unable worms!
My mind hath been as big as one of yours,
My heart as great, my reason haply more,
To bandy word for word and frown for frown;
But now I see our lances are but straws,
Our strength as weak, our weakness past compare,
That seeming to be most which we indeed least are.
Then vail your stomachs,[8] for it is no boot,[9]
And place your hands below your husband's foot:
In token of which duty, if he please,
My hand is ready, may it do him ease.

PET. Why, there 's a wench! Come on, and kiss me, Kate.

LUC. Well, go thy ways, old lad; for thou shalt ha 't.

VIN. 'T is a good hearing, when children are toward.

LUC. But a harsh hearing, when women are froward.

PET. Come, Kate, we 'll to bed.
We three are married, but you two are sped.[10]
'T was I won the wager, though you hit the white;[11] [*To Lucentio.*
And, being a winner, God give you good night!

[*Exeunt Petruchio and Katharina.*

HOR. Now, go thy ways; thou hast tamed a curst shrew.

LUC. 'T is a wonder, by your leave, she will be tamed so. [*Exeunt.*

[7] *soft conditions*] gentle qualities (of mind).

[8] *vail your stomachs*] abate your pride.

[9] *it is no boot*] there is no advantage.

[10] *you two are sped*] you two are undone, done for.

[11] *hit the white*] hit the bull's eye, with a play on Bianca's name, which is the Italian word for "white."